150 TIPS AND TRICKS FOR

New Nurses

✓ Find a healthy work-to-life balance
✓ Develop good patient and coworker relations
✓ Stay informed in this ever-changing field

Kathy Quan, RN, BSN, PHN

Aadamsmedia
Avon, Massachusetts

Contains material adapted and abridged from *The Everything® New Nurse
Book*, by Kathy Quan, RN, BSN, PHN, © 2006 by F+W Publications, Inc., ISBN
10: 1-59337-532-8, ISBN 13: 978-1-59337-532-4.

Published by
Adams Media, a division of F+W Media, Inc.
57 Littlefield Street, Avon, MA 02322. U.S.A.
www.adamsmedia.com

ISBN 10: 1-59869-776-5
ISBN 13: 978-1-59869-776-6
Printed in the United States of America.

J I H G F E D C B A

Library of Congress Cataloging-in-Publication Data
is available from the publisher.

This publication is designed to provide accurate and authoritative information
with regard to the subject matter covered. It is sold with the understanding that
the publisher is not engaged in rendering legal, accounting, or other professional
advice. If legal advice or other expert assistance is required, the services of a
competent professional person should be sought.
　—From a *Declaration of Principles* jointly adopted by a Committee of the
American Bar Association and a Committee of Publishers and Associations

Many of the designations used by manufacturers and sellers to distinguish their
product are claimed as trademarks. Where those designations appear in this
book and Adams Media was aware of a trademark claim, the designations have
been printed with initial capital letters.

This book is available at quantity discounts for bulk purchases.
For information, please call 1-800-289-0963.

Contents

Introduction

The Professional Caregiver

Welcome to the world of nursing. As you embark on your new career, know that you have made a wise and wonderful choice to give of yourself to help make a difference in someone's life every day. Nursing is one of the most rewarding and yet challenging careers. Nursing can be a thankless job, but at the same time, it can bring you countless hours of joy and some of the most heartfelt love.

Nursing is one of the most physically and emotionally demanding careers. You will require a great deal of physical stamina and a strong sense of humor to perform your daily duties. Nurses combine the art of caring with a strong scientific knowledge base to provide care, promote wellness, and improve the lives of their patients. It takes strong communication skills, both written and oral, combined with a scientific mind and a warm heart and soul to form the foundation for a good nurse.

This book is based on the experiences of many nurses and is meant to help you to understand that you are not alone in your feelings at any stage in your career. Every nurse was once a new grad. Every nurse has had just as many firsts as you will:

first patient, first shot, first birth, first death, first error, first special moment when it all makes sense. Share in their triumphs and failures as you grow into one of the finest professions.

Always remember to recharge your own batteries. Take care of yourself so that you have the strength and stamina and desire to care for others who need you. Learn from your mistakes and move on. Enjoy your career and always keep track of your accomplishments and successes. Find something positive about every day. If you ever lose track of why you became a nurse, think back to these moments and your doubts will fade. Good luck and thank you for becoming a nurse.

Part One

The Responsibilities of a New Nurse

A nurse is a professional caregiver—
someone who advocates for patient's rights,
promotes health, educates patients and
families, and strives to eliminate pain and
suffering. A nurse has a great responsibility
for the care and treatment of her patients.
Nursing is one of the most rewarding
professions, and yet at times can be one
of the most frustrating and thankless jobs.
A nurse is a highly skilled individual who
learns to combine the scientific aspect of
health care with the fine art of caring.

1   Pick the Type of Nurse You Want to Be

A Registered Nurse (RN) is a nurse who has graduated with a diploma or a degree from a state-approved nursing program, passed the state board examination for professional nurses, and has been granted a license by the state to practice professional nursing in that state. RNs with advanced degrees and certificates will have increased options for their scope of practice. A Licensed Practical (or Vocational) Nurse (LPN/LVN) is a technical nurse who has graduated from a state-approved nursing program, passed the state board examination for practical nursing, and has been granted a license to practice in that state as a practical nurse. The LPN/LVN works under the supervision of an RN or a physician to provide patient care. With IV Certification, the LPN/LVN can perform certain aspects of IV care. The title of Practical or Vocational Nurse varies by state law, but the role is essentially the same.

One role is the practical nurse, sometimes referred to as the technical nurse. This is the LPN/LVN. The other is the professional nurse. This is the RN. Both play an essential part as members of the health care team. Their roles and responsibilities vary. An RN can perform any of the duties of an LPN, but the reverse is not true.

In some instances, an LVN's skills at specific tasks may be more refined than those of her supervising RN. This can often be the case because the LVN has the primary responsibility for performing bedside nursing and tasks, while the RN is given a supervisory responsibility for the patient's care and often forgoes the hands-on practice of direct patient care.

RN training involves more science, math, patient assessment, critical thinking, and theoretical aspects than does the training of an LPN/LVN. This includes the nursing process, which encompasses the whole patient and his response to his illness as well as to patient treatment.

Remember to "Do No Harm"

All nurses promise to do no harm to any patient and are expected to uphold fundamental responsibilities to help to prevent illness and restore health, to help to alleviate pain and suffering, and to promote health. Nurses should also follow a code of ethics for nurses as set and frequently revised by the American Nurses Association (ANA). The International Council of Nurses (ICN) has also written a code of ethics for nurses that expands on the ANA's code.

Highlights of the responsibilities and guidelines for the ethical and legal practice of nurses as outlined in these codes are:

- The nurse is expected to provide care for a patient with respect for his human dignity and uniqueness as an individual regardless of race, creed, gender, socio-economic status, or the nature of the illness.
- The nurse is responsible for safeguarding the patient's right to privacy by honoring the confidentiality of information related to the patient.
- The nurse is responsible for protecting her patient and the public from health and safety issues affected by illegal, incompetent, and unethical practices.

- The nurse is responsible and accountable for her own nursing actions and judgments, as well as for those she is supervising.
- The nurse is responsible for maintaining her own nursing competency.
- The nurse is responsible for making informed decisions about her own skills and abilities as well as for those to whom she might delegate the responsibility. The nurse is expected to seek consultation if necessary before accepting or delegating the responsibility for any aspect of a patient's care.
- The nurse is expected to participate in the nursing profession's ongoing efforts and activities to expand the core of research-based knowledge for nurses. The nurse is expected to participate in the nursing profession's efforts to implement and improve the standards of nursing care.
- The nurse is expected to participate in the nursing profession's efforts to maintain conditions of employment, including equitable socio-economic standards, which allow for delivery of high-quality nursing care.

- The nurse is responsible for participating with the nursing profession in protecting the public from misinformation and misrepresentations.

The nursing profession is not to be taken lightly, nor to be entered into on a whim. Nurses are the backbone of the health care team. Nurses render health care not only to the individual patients, but also to their families and to the community. Nurses are expected to coordinate the efforts of everyone involved to enhance the health and well-being of their patients. Nurses are responsible for respecting human rights. These include the right to life, the right to dignity, and the right to respect.

Many patient safety rules or goals are based on pure common sense. Some are more elaborate. Each institution will have variations of its own rules and goals based on mistakes others have made and their attempts to prevent a reoccurrence. Others will be based on preventing common errors based on data collected by organizations such as Joint Commission on Accreditation of Healthcare Organizations (JCAHO), whose goal is to advocate for quality and safety for all.

As a licensed nurse, your responsibility is to promote health and well-being. Under the Nurse Practice Act (NPA) for your state, you will find a section that deals with disciplinary measures. Here, you will most likely find that not only will you be punished by the laws of your state for the DUI, but that your nursing license is subject to suspension or revocation. This is true even though you were not on duty at the time of the DUI.

The commission of other criminal acts, not limited to malpractice issues or the illegal use of drugs, can also result in the suspension or revocation of your nursing license. These acts can include things such as writing bad checks, shoplifting, fraud, and so on. Remember, you are a professional person, and you are expected to conduct yourself in a professional manner at all times.

Know Your Scope of Practice

Each member of the health care team is allowed to perform certain duties based on the content and level of education received, the license granted, and the specifics of the laws and regulations of the state in which they are practicing.

No matter what level of nursing you are functioning at, it is always in your own interest, as well as the patient's best interest, to understand each person's scope of practice. If you are the aide or the LVN, you aren't responsible for, nor expected to assess and analyze, the data. However, it can be in everyone's best interest to have an understanding of what other symptoms might be important to report and why. This can be especially important and helpful in the event of short-staffing. Concise communication is vital to quality patient care. If you are ever in doubt, it is always best to ask for assistance or another opinion. To err on the side of safety is always best.

The Nurse Practice Act (NPA) is the group of laws in a state that protect the public health. It defines the scope of practice for nurses in that state. The Nurse Practice Act (NPA) also includes the requirements for education and licensing, as well as disciplinary and punitive measures for unsafe practice. It is the responsibility of every nurse to know the responsibilities and limitations outlined in the NPA of the state(s) in which the nurse practices.

It is the responsibility of each licensed nurse to read and to know the contents of his own Nurse Practice Act (NPA). The NPA will be different for RNs, LPNs, and APRNs (advance practice RNs). You will be held accountable for this information. Read the NPA and understand it. If you have questions, ask. Your board of nurses is there to answer your questions and to help you to understand your scope of practice.

Part One: The Responsibilities of a New Nurse

Be a Nursing Ambassador

Remember that you represent the nursing profession at all times—whether at work or at play. Your attire, hygiene, actions, and demeanor are always on display. This can be an intense responsibility and unfair at times, perhaps, but something you must be aware of.

In addition to representing the nursing profession, whether on or off duty you represent your employer. How you appear and act reflects on the employer's business. If you conduct yourself professionally and present a professional demeanor, you will command the respect you deserve from your employer, your coworkers, your patients, families, and community.

If you look and act the role, your patients will have much more respect for you as a professional. You will be much better able to convince them that what you are telling them is in their best interest. You will gain your patients' confidence and be much better able to educate them and advocate for them.

Doctors have the advantage of having a longer-term relationship with a patient than most nurses. Doctors will see the patient from the initial diagnosis through to the cure or through the course of long-term treatment. Doctors receive their emotional rewards when the patient is cured or learns to cope with an illness and make the appropriate lifestyle changes.

Nurses are a part of this process as well, except that they never diagnose. (In some instances, nurse practitioners who have been specifically trained to do so can diagnose illnesses in patients, but as a rule, nurses do not diagnose.) They collaborate with the physician and coordinate the scientific information about the disease with the patient's ability to cope, to understand, and to respond to the treatment. The nurse usually has a more limited experience with the patient according to where she practices. This might be a two- to four-day hospital stay and the nurse has a short time to participate in the care.

Part One: The Responsibilities of a New Nurse

9. Remember Why You Became a Nurse

"Why not become a doctor?" This is the burning question that at least one of your loved ones or best friends will probably ask you, and not just once, but many times over. You may even ask it of yourself. The answer, however, will be a personal one. The health care team is composed of doctors, nurses, therapists, social workers, nursing assistants, pharmacists, and a whole ancillary staff of nonlicensed personnel. Why not become a doctor? Because you want to be a nurse.

"Why do you want to be a nurse?" This is another one of those nagging questions from well-meaning friends and loved ones. You can usually explain yourself and move on. When someone asks you why you would want to be a nurse, the answer is that you want to make a difference in the quality of someone's life every day!

Those who choose medicine as a career do so because they want to help people, but more so because they want to be involved in the diagnosis and treatment of disease. They want to be part of the act of curing someone. Doctors have the advantage of having a longer term relationship with a patient than most nurses. Doctors will see the patient from the initial diagnosis through to the cure or through the course of long-term treatment. They receive their emotional rewards when the patient is cured or learns to cope with an illness and make the appropriate life-style changes.

Nurses are a part of this process as well, except that they never diagnose. (In some instances, nurse practitioners who have been specifically trained to do so can diagnose illnesses in patients, but as a rule, nurses do not diagnose.) They collaborate with the physician and coordinate the scientific information about the disease with the patient's ability to cope, to understand, and to respond to the treatment. The nurse usually has a more limited experience with the patient according to where she practices. This might be a two- to four-day hospital stay and the nurse has a short time to participate in the care. Consequently, the nurse may not see the full results of her efforts, while the doctor will.

Nurses Educate and Advocate

Nurses look at the patient as a whole and make a nursing diagnosis, a standardized statement with regard to the disease and what else is needed to help the patient cope and respond to the treatment. This includes lifestyle issues, nutrition, and hygiene, as well as knowledge deficits. Armed with all this information, the nurse sets out to educate the patient about his illness, the treatment modalities necessary, and the expected response. The nurse also helps the patient to understand any possible side effects and untoward signs and symptoms that should be reported to the doctor.

Nurses also work independently to provide case management, develop care standards, and improve the quality of patient care. Additionally, they educate patients and family members about aspects of health and wellness, taking responsibility for the patients' own health and promoting awareness of health care issues.

Nursing at all levels, whether as an LPN, an RN, or an APRN, is a profession. Achieving this status has been a hard-fought battle that all nurses must continue to fight with the goal of attracting more capable young people into the profession.

The nursing profession is not to be taken lightly, nor to be entered into on a whim. Nurses are the backbone of the health care team. Nurses render health care not only to the individual patients, but also to their families and to the community. Nurses are expected to coordinate the efforts of everyone involved to enhance the health and well-being of their patients. Nurses are responsible for respecting human rights. These include the right to life, the right to dignity, and the right to respect.

Take the Good and the Bad

Nursing is one of the most rewarding professions for those who love people and love helping people. The roles for nurses are always expanding, which keeps the field new and exciting. Technology and advances in medical science offer new and challenging opportunities to work on the cutting edge of science. There are an unlimited number of career choices in nursing.

There are also drawbacks. Patients don't always say "thank you." The job is physically, emotionally, and mentally challenging. Patients need nurses on weekends and holidays and at all hours of the day and night. The growing shortage of nurses is due in part to the fact that nurses often lack respect in the work force. Nurses are overworked and underpaid. That is a fact, but salaries are increasing and work conditions are improving.

Basic computer skills are essential to almost any career now, and nursing is no exception. You will need word processing skills and a good understanding of how to research topics on the Internet in order to survive college or vocational school. Health care is rapidly becoming automated, from programmable pumps for IVs to computerized medical records. A comfort level in utilizing computers is essential for anyone pursuing a nursing career today.

Technology is going to rapidly come to the forefront of efforts to improve patients' safety and access to health care and outcomes, as well as to contain costs. The Internet can provide you with all sorts of information, such as the latest news on recent discoveries about diagnoses, treatments, and outcomes. You can access information about support groups and organizations that support research. You can find information about health care legislation being proposed and voted on. You can join listservs and receive updates and discussions via e-mail. Just make sure that the sources for your information are well known and qualified!

All Nurses Are "Real" Nurses

You will encounter many different attitudes about nurses. One of them is the strong belief by some that only hospital nurses are "real nurses." Another is that LPNs are inferior and not really nurses at all. All nurses are an essential part of the overall health care picture. Many times you'll find LPNs whose skills and bedside manners are impeccable and who best teach the new nursing grads and physicians how to perform the most technical procedures. The argument should never be about who is better, but rather about who is the most professional. The most professional nurse is the one who sees all nurses as necessary parts of the whole; she recognizes the contributions of their individual special talents and skills to the team effort and that they strive to make a difference in someone's life every day. Whether the nurse's role is direct care or a supportive role behind the scenes, all roles are necessary and vital to providing patients with improved outcomes.

There are many roles for nurses. Inside the hospital arena, these include, but are not limited to, staff nurses, surgical nurses, midwives, lactation specialists, rehab nurses, nurse anesthetists, IV specialists, staff educators, supervisors, clinical specialists, clinical managers, quality and utilization specialists, nursing directors, and administrators.

Outside the hospital, there are many other roles, such as clinic nurses, office nurses, school nurses, forensic nurses, industrial nurses, case managers for insurance companies and worker's compensation, sales reps for drugs and medical supplies, clinical research nurses, diabetic educators, wound ostomy nurses, legal nurse consultants, flight nurses, childbirth educators, dialysis nurses, home health nurses, hospice nurses, and private duty nurses. There are managers and health care administrators and many, many more. Travel nurses fill vacancies in all areas, primarily in hospitals and clinics, but their roles are expanding as well.

Part Two

Starting Off on the Right Foot

Think about some of the hospitals where you have done your clinical rotations. Which one might offer you the best opportunity to spend at least your first year gathering all the experience you can get? If you took the opportunity for an externship program as a student, you may have gleaned some valuable insight into finding an employer who is going to offer you the best place to spend your first year as a nurse.

Work at a Large Teaching Hospital

The one advantage of the nursing shortage is that you can find a job almost anywhere. Take advantage of it and get the best experience you can in your first year. Then the whole world of nursing will be wide open to you. If at all possible, one of the best places to train is a hospital associated with a medical school. By the same token, your first job as a nurse in one of these facilities can be one of the best experiences you may have in your career. Patients in a teaching hospital are primed for students, and these patients have a good understanding of the culture in a learning environment. These facilities often have more funds available to afford the most state-of-the-art equipment. The doctors are usually well versed in the latest in procedures and treatments. You will be exposed to patients with far more complex diseases and those having experimental treatments.

You don't have to be a hospital nurse forever, but you do need to have a solid foundation of skills, and the best place to get that is in a hospital. If you have worked as an aide for a year or more, have had the opportunity to observe procedures and treatments, and have had a very strong clinical education, you might not need as much experience. However, nurses and even physicians don't learn everything they need to know in school.

If you had an externship in the hospital during your schooling, you might also be well prepared. And if you are going to have an internship in another facility or environment, you might be ready to move into another area of nursing. Of course, if you are an LPN who has completed an RN program, you should be able to move into another role more easily as well.

Part Two: Starting Off on the Right Foot

18 Get a Strong General Background

Once you have a strong foundation of experience in basic nursing care for adults, you can branch out into more specialized care, and you will have options to go anywhere in your career. You will always have the confidence that you have developed skills and seen and done a wide variety of procedures successfully. If you don't have this opportunity, opt for the most general experience you can get in your area. No matter how much experience you may have gained in school, a good solid foundation as a generalist will give you the tools to build your career in any area of nursing.

One of the reasons most nurses leave nursing is because of burnout and feeling trapped with nowhere to go because they are too specialized and making a change would take too much re-education. This seems to be especially true for those wishing to move from something like pediatrics into adult care.

A general background will give you both the experience and the credibility to be able to move laterally and to move upward. The additional advantage is that even after a long career in a highly specialized area, most nurses with a strong generalist foundation will find the courage to move into a whole new realm much more often than those who headed straight to their specialty area after graduation and stayed there for ten years. These nurses tend to feel trapped because they have been pigeonholed and don't have a general background to fall back on.

The nurse with the general med-surg (medical/surgical) background has many opportunities to move directly out of the hospital into areas such as clinics, home health, and case management. With some additional training or an internship in a specialized area, he can move into a multitude of areas, such as ICU, pediatrics, rehab, oncology, women's health, and clinical trials.

Be Aware of Options Outside the Hospital

There are many different roles and career options for nurses beyond the hospital setting, and you may have had some exposure to them either from clinical rotations or through previous careers. In many of these fields, you will most likely have more autonomy, and you will likely have fewer nurse colleagues around to help when you encounter a situation you are unsure of. You need to have a solid foundation of skills, including assessment and critical thinking skills, in order to provide the best quality care to your patients. A hospital experience can expose you to more than you may ever need to know, but it can also help to assure that you can face any situation with confidence and skill for at least basic care until more advanced help can be accessed. Be aware, however, that many positions require, if not highly recommend, one year's recent acute hospital experience.

These incentives are not always cash offers, but they can include cars, housekeepers, housing assistance, babysitters, and so on. There are offers for nurses to come in and write their own ticket, so to speak. However, these enticements don't come without strings. Please be sure to read the fine print and be prepared to work for this employer for a set length of time in return for this reward.

Investigate the day care centers, check out the dealership providing the car, and talk to the nurses to see if they have gotten what they asked for in writing their own plans. What are the terms for the cash outlay? Do you get it all up front, or do you have to wait for the term to be up before you get the majority of the money? Proceed with your eyes open and a full understanding of all the terms before you jump headfirst into something you might later regret.

Check Your Equipment

If your stethoscope from school was cheap and is worn out, treat yourself to a new one. You deserve it. If you're going to be working in a specialty unit, you may need a more expensive and specialized model, but check with the other nurses on the unit for advice first. They may have information about discounts and opinions about one model over another.

Make sure that your other equipment is clean and in good working condition. If your scissors are dull or rusty, be sure to clean and sharpen them or replace them. If your pocket flashlight doesn't have replaceable batteries, check it. If it's no longer bright, toss it out and replace it. Try to find one with replaceable batteries and light bulbs and keep extras in your locker.

Be sure you always have in your pocket a pen that writes. A pocket holder for your pen, scissors, clamps, and flashlight is always handy.

A big must is an up-to-date edition of some sort of drug book or drug software. You must always use the most recent edition of a drug book, and you should always discard the old ones. New drugs won't be in your four-year-old edition.

Read your drug book and become familiar with it so that it is easy for you to use quickly. Understand how drugs are cross-referenced, how to find side effects, and what the nursing implications are for each drug. Know how to find the tables that list sound-alike drugs. Keep this book with you at all times and use it. Never give a medication you are unfamiliar with under any circumstances. Never take a verbal order for a medication without repeating it back to the physician and verifying that it is indeed the drug she is prescribing. Then look it up. If you have questions, refer to the pharmacist for assistance.

You could also get a PDA—they can be lifesavers! It's smaller than a drug book and can contain a vast amount of important information which is available at the touch of a button. The software has search capabilities to provide quicker access. The initial investment can be less than $100 and has the option of adding on more memory and accessories as needed.

PDA stands for personal digital assistant. It is virtually a hand-held computer. Most are about three inches by five inches and about one-half inch thick. The PDA comes with a small device called a stylus that acts like a pencil and a pointing device.

The PDA is a personal organizer, address book, calendar, to-do list, calculator, and memo/note pad all in one small pocket device. It can house databases and hook up to the Internet for Web surfing and e-mail. Some include voice recorders and cell phones. Accessories can be added to make it serve as an MP3 player. A small keyboard can be attached to use in lieu of the built-in touch pad.

You need shoes that will provide a strong, sturdy base for ensuring your own safety. You need to set your feet to bend your knees and get the leverage you need to lift and transfer patients and to move beds and equipment. You will often have to run and frequently to move quickly. Perhaps most important of all, you'll need a shoe with a nonslip sole. Your shoes can make or break your day. Invest wisely. Many nurses prefer a clog-type shoe made of soft PVC. These often have an ergonomic design to the sole that offers good foot and back support. You may also find it helpful to have two or three different shoe types and to trade them off. When they get worn down on the sides or heels, you'll need to replace them to maximize your comfort and support, as well as your safety.

Part Two: Starting Off on the Right Foot

Before your first day, you should know what time you need to be there, what you need to bring, and what type of orientation you'll have. Come prepared, arrive early, and take a moment to relax. Be sure to pack a lunch and a snack just in case you can't find anything in the cafeteria that you can eat. If you're not working in a hospital, you may not have an opportunity to go out for a meal, or perhaps everyone eats in.

You'll need to bring with you any paperwork you were given. This might include forms you need to return, an employee handbook, your job description, and anything they asked you to bring when you were hired. Always carry your driver's license, nursing license (if you have it), CPR card, and copies of any certificates you have received. Unless you have already provided your social security card, you may need to have this with you as well. Employers must see the card.

In most cases, your first day will be an orientation. Although this may be an all-day orientation, you should come prepared with your nursing equipment unless you were told otherwise. This should include your watch, stethoscope, bandage scissors, pocket flashlight and pen in a pocket holder, and a new edition drug book or PDA with up-to-date pharmacology software. All items should be clearly labeled with your name and contact information.

As you meet people and tour the facility, try to get an idea of the culture. How are people addressed? Who is introduced with most formality? Remember to make a good first impression on those you meet. Smile, shake hands when possible, make eye contact, be friendly, and try to make an association of the name and face with what department they work in. You won't remember everyone, but at least you'll recognize a few of them.

Part Two: Starting Off on the Right Foot

Pay Attention and Take Notes

You may be in orientation for the facility for several weeks or months and that may be split with time on your unit. In any case, you will also have an orientation to your own unit. Pay close attention to all orientations you attend and take notes. Review your notes and any handouts you were given each day.

You will also be instructed in the documentation policies. If the facility uses a different format for charting than you have been exposed to, be sure you ask for additional help as you go along. Never assume that you'll catch on later. Documentation is too important to let slide. Depending on the extent that computers are used in your facility, you will be oriented to their use as well. Not all computer programs are created equal, so if you need additional instruction, be sure to ask for it now.

Your orientation will most likely be during the day shift, whether or not that is the shift you were hired for. You may be mixed with new hires from all disciplines or separated into only nurses. This might even be just new grads or a mix with all newly hired nurses.

Get to know as many of your fellow new hires as you can. The medical world is very small and you'll never know when and where you may be working with someone again in the future. You are all new and nervous and a friendly gesture will be remembered and appreciated.

Orientation is the time to work out as many kinks and bugs as you can. The nurse educators are there just for this purpose. If you wait and think you'll learn it later, you may regret it. When you're working on the floor, you should never do something you are unsure of without asking for help. However, if this was something you should have learned in orientation, your coworkers may not be too happy with you. If you just need a little reassurance, that's one thing, but if you fail to utilize orientation to learn all that you can, your coworkers will resent it.

During orientation, you will be introduced to the policies and procedures for your facility. You will also be shown how to use the various pieces of equipment and pumps used within the facility. You will spend time on clinical issues, and you may at this time begin being checked off on procedures. This is the time to ask lots of questions and to speak up if there is something you are not comfortable with or have not done before.

Some of the most important items you need to locate are your reference manuals, including your policy and procedure manual (often referred to as the P&P) and your standards of care manual. Learn the specific protocols your facility has regarding things such as central line care. And are there any doctors who have their own specific protocol that differs from facility protocols? Watch and learn. Ask questions. Don't ever assume. Use your time wisely. Make yourself an asset to your unit.

Make note of where things such as the crash cart, fire extinguishers, central supplies, and linens are located. Learn how your medication cart is laid out and how it works. Even if you aren't allowed to dispense medications or controlled substances, know how it is done. You should know how to access the meds if the system is computerized and how to get a newly prescribed medication from the pharmacy.

Know how to obtain procedure trays and central supplies. How do you charge the patient for the supplies you use? What happens if you or someone else contaminates a sterile tray and you need to get another one? Is there a charge-off procedure? How do you order the lab work, x-rays, or other tests the doctor has just requested for her patient? How do you access the lab and test results? What about IVs? Is there an IV team? Do the interns and residents start new IVs? Where are the IV sets kept?

Part Three

Handling On-the-Job Issues

Come to work prepared. Have all your equipment ready to go. If you have a locker, leave things at work so they aren't forgotten on the table at home or left in your car. If you don't have a place to leave them, then carry a backpack or other tote bag to keep them all organized. Start the day with a smile and a positive attitude. Greet your coworkers with a warm hello. But don't overdo it. Be sincere and address people by name.

Put Your Best Foot Forward

As the new kid on the block, you're going to annoy someone—whether it's another nurse or the unit secretary doesn't make much difference. There always will be people who have little patience for someone new. Or perhaps they had a bad start to their day or aren't feeling up to par. Try to apologize for whatever you did to annoy them and later come back and try to work it out calmly. Sometimes, you just have to ignore it and learn not to take things personally.

Compliment coworkers on a job well done. If a patient tells you something nice about another nurse, pass the comment along to the nurse and even to your supervisor. All your coworkers are resources. Those who have been there the longest can be very valuable in educating you on the culture, history, and traditions of the facility and your particular unit.

As you transition out of orientation and into your regular assignment, expect to be treated like the new guy. You'll have to earn the respect of your new coworkers. You'll have to prove yourself to be accepted as one of the team.

In a setting where the staff is especially short-handed, it can be an added stress to the older staff members to have new nurses who need additional help and supervision. You may also encounter some issues of professional jealousy.

Don't be discouraged; you will also meet many new friends and allies. You will find a mentor and learn many tricks and tips to help you provide excellent patient care throughout your nursing career. You can help improve this situation if you pay close attention to where things are so that you don't have to ask more than once or twice.

Accept the Demands of Being the Newbie

You haven't been jaded by some of the "revolving door" or "frequent flier" patients who can drive nurses mad. They will be sure to share the wealth with you by giving you all the patients they have burned out on or need a break from. This isn't always a bad thing, but it can be challenging to you as a new nurse. You'll bring new interest and knowledge to the situation and may find a way to help the patient better than anyone has in a long time. Don't be surprised if not everyone applauds your success though. Someone just might take offense or claim that you're just showing off.

You may also find yourself with most of the grunt work assignments for maintaining the unit. And if there is a particular employee who isn't well liked, you can be sure you'll be partnered with that person as often as possible.

Unless you look seventy or older, you're going to be told over and over that you're too young to be a nurse. Some patients will mean it as a compliment and others will be frightened and worried that you don't know what you're doing. The patient might think that you haven't had enough experience and might ask you to please not touch her. You will need to reassure her that indeed you have graduated from an accredited school of nursing and that you have been trained to perform whatever it is you are doing.

If you need to do something that you haven't done before, be honest and let the patient know that your preceptor is right there. If you're just being checked off on the procedure, let her know you have performed this before, but it's hospital policy that your preceptor check you off before you can do it alone— it's just standard procedure.

Part Three: Handling On-the-Job Issues

Never Be Afraid to Ask

You need to complete your assignments and to communicate clearly with your coworkers at all times. If you need to leave the floor, you report off to someone who will cover for you. If you have questions, you need to be sure to ask them. Don't be intimidated by the other nurses. They have more experience than you have right now, but you have worked just as hard to become a nurse. You will find that asking questions does not make you look stupid or ignorant, but rather shows a desire to learn and a respect for your coworkers' knowledge and ability. In health care, learning is an ongoing process for everyone.

If you haven't done something or are uncomfortable with a procedure, ask for help. Be honest; don't try to bluff your way through something, even in the event that you find yourself alone with a physician who expects you to assist him.

Look to the resources around you for answers. Social workers and therapists (physical, occupational, respiratory, and speech) deal with the same patients you do. These other staff members may have an entirely different perspective on the care a patient needs. Sometimes patients respond to them in a different way, either positively or negatively, for various reasons. A patient may be combative with the nurse who is trying to administer medication or perform a procedure, but he may be totally cooperative with the physical therapist who's helping him to walk.

It is also helpful to learn the role that each discipline plays on the health care team. Nurses tend to believe that they have total responsibility for the patient and need to understand how and when to delegate. If you have a better understanding of the part each team member plays, you will also be less likely to overstep and interfere with the total plan of care.

Maintain a Professional Appearance

All nurses need to strive for maintaining a professional appearance at all times. Caps and white starched uniforms may be a thing of the past, but there is no excuse for dressing inappropriately. No matter what setting you work in, clean, professional attire must be worn. Wearing clean surgical scrubs and lab coats goes a long way toward distinguishing nurses as health care professionals. These clothes are not expensive, and should be laundered regularly. Your appearance will be graded by your coworkers, your employer, and your patients. If you look like a nurse, you'll gain respect from everyone. Your clothes should be clean and wrinkle-free. You should be clean and impeccably groomed.

Nursing is a conservative field in the sense that flashy, fashionable dress is really not appropriate. This is true even in roles where nurses can wear street clothes as opposed to a uniform. Keep to the basics of clean fresh uniforms and modest jewelry for work.

Infection control is affected by your personal grooming issues. Having your hair fall into your field of vision in the middle of a procedure can be a cause for concern. Not only does hair falling in your face present the potential for you to make a mistake, but also it can contaminate your clean or sterile field. Having to brush your hair aside can cause you to break technique, contaminate yourself, or require you to remove yourself in the middle of a procedure to wash and reglove. All these put you and the patient at risk.

Long fingernails, whether natural or artificial, and jewelry such as rings have long been known to harbor bacteria even with the best hand-washing efforts. Using gloves can alleviate the infection risk, but the practical approach is to keep nails short and hair short or pulled back and to limit or omit jewelry in the workplace. This is for your protection as well as for the patient's protection

Minimize Perfume and Smoke

When considering whether to wear scented shaving lotions, perfumes, hair products, or mouthwash, nurses should remember that they work with sick people. The sense of smell of an ill person may be more acute because of medications and treatments such as chemotherapy. The sensitivity to smells may also be heightened due to allergies, migraines, and other aspects of illness and intolerance.

Smoking is another consideration. If you smoke, you smell of smoke. Your skin, your hair, and your clothing can reek no matter how well you try to mask it. Sometimes the masking only increases the potency of the smell. Just because you are not smoking in the presence of patients doesn't mean your smoking is not a problem. Everywhere your cigarettes have been, the smell of smoke has been there too. Your car, your purse, and your clothes will all smell of smoke. Be aware of this and try to minimize the experience for others.

Come to work on time. That means you should arrive and be ready to work at your scheduled time, not just rushing to clock in at the exact moment. Give yourself about fifteen minutes to put away your belongings, get a cup of coffee, and greet your coworkers. If you plan on this extra time, then if you occasionally encounter heavier traffic or other unforeseen situations, you should still arrive on time.

Don't call in sick unless you really are. Nursing is not a job that can wait to be done until you get there tomorrow. If you're not there for your scheduled shift, everyone else is going to have to pick up some of your work along with their own. Of course, if you are harboring germs, please keep them to yourself and don't share them with your coworkers and patients.

In many instances, the blood you've been exposed to is either yours or that of a close friend or loved one. The sight of your own blood has usually involved pain. Your body's response incorporates a natural defense mechanism and you may feel faint or nauseated as a result.

When a friend or loved one is injured, your emotional response incorporates this mechanism and you may have the same type of response. This is not to say you won't have the same response to a stranger's blood, but it should be less of an issue. It is something that you can and will develop a level of tolerance to given time. Additionally, as a nurse you will often automatically move into an "emergency/help mode," and you won't really have time to worry about your own response.

And if needles terrify you, just remember, as the nurse, you won't be on the receiving end. Learning to handle and use hypodermics and IV needles prior to injecting a patient will help you to have a new respect for needles. As an instrument to help you assist the patient in getting well or alleviating pain, needles will take on a different meaning to you.

In fact, your own fears will help you to be a better nurse. You'll wield the needles with more compassion and you'll be sure to take the time to help the patient tolerate the procedure better.

If you can't stand the smell of hospitals, your intolerance is probably linked to a scary or unpleasant experience in a hospital. As a student and then as a nurse, your experience will change the way you think about hospitals. As with anything else, the more time you spend around an odor, the less you can smell it. At first, you may find that everything smells like the hospital, and then that sensation will begin to fade. As you spend time in the hospital and understand what makes some of the smells, your fears will fade as well.

There is a common misperception that the smells are emanating from sick people, but, in fact, it is usually a combination of cleaning chemicals, food odors, plants and flowers of all varieties, a multitude of perfumes and body scents, and so many people congregating in a space that has no open windows.

If you pass out at the sight of an open wound, your emotional response combined with your body's defense mechanisms is most likely causing you to faint. If someone else has already seen the wound you are about to go and re-dress, ask that person what it looks like. If you already have a vision in your mind, you'll be more prepared for what you find. Surprises can make the experience a lot worse. Read the chart, what was the latest description? Are there any photos in there? Be prepared, and it won't be as bad as you anticipated.

Wounds, especially large, infected ones, are not a favorite of any nurse. Wound ostomy nurses (WOCNs and RN ETs) who specialize in wound care seem to be more tolerant and can even discuss them over meals, but in general this is something that you will develop your own way of coping with.

Use Gum or Mints to Mask Unpleasant Smells

If you gag at the sight of excrement and bodily secretions, it's usually the smell that gets to you. Doing something to avoid or mask the smell can help. Breathing through your mouth helps. You can also cough. It's impossible to cough and gag at the same time.

One way of dealing with unpleasant smells is to use a little camphor or eucalyptus oil on the tip of your nose to mask the smell until you become more comfortable in a hospital setting. Another suggestion for helping to disguise unpleasant odors and to keep from gagging is to pop a hard candy or cough drop with a strong menthol, mint, or cinnamon flavor in your mouth just before you go into the room. Gum with a strong flavor will help as well, but the taste may not last as long as the candy's.

When it comes to staffing for holidays, expect to be working the main ones. Remember, sick people don't suddenly get well for the holidays. Those nurses with seniority have already paid their dues and will expect you to do so now. In fact, it may take several years before you spend Christmas Day with your family. Memorial Day may just become your favorite holiday and one of the few you might actually get off. Of course, you'll have an alternate day off during that week as your "paid holiday," which can have its advantages.

Spending a holiday with your patients can be a warm and rewarding experience. This is especially true with those patients who are alone or who may have been recently widowed. Making a difference in someone's life every day takes on an even more special meaning at such times. New nurses usually find this especially rewarding.

Part Four

Teamwork Works

Learn to accept your role as a team member.
Support your coworkers where they fall short
and step up to the plate when needed to
lead the group. United you will succeed.
Separately you might not be effective. The
goal is to enrich the life of the patient, not
to promote your self-worth. The rewards you
reap will come in the form of satisfaction
not for becoming a superstar but for having
played a part in making a difference in
someone's life today.

Be Aware of Office Politics

The political climate and culture of your unit should be set by the management, but sometimes it is the "old guard" or long-timers who seem to have an upper hand in the way things get done. That isn't to say that the management isn't effective or is too soft. It just usually means that there are one or two staff members who have a strong sense of entitlement because they have been there forever. They have paid their dues and get first choice at the perks, such as holidays and scheduled meal breaks. Sometimes they are RNs and sometimes they are nursing assistants, so it isn't always rank that gets or expects the privileges.

Your best option as the new kid on the block is to sit back, listen, and observe. You'll learn whom you can trust and around whom you need to be very careful what you say.

Don't get caught up in the gossip, but pay attention to what is being said and by whom to avoid becoming a topic yourself. Understand the lay of the land. Gossip is an inherent part of almost every workplace. You may not be able to avoid it. You won't have enough information as a new member of the staff to distinguish all that is true and what isn't, so it's best to try not to make judgments based on what you hear. Give people the benefit of the doubt and form your own opinions based on firsthand experiences. Try to be fair and equal in your treatment of all your coworkers. Look for the good in everyone and avoid bad-mouthing anyone.

If you have a conflict, try to be direct and discuss it calmly and rationally in private with the person(s) involved. If you can't resolve it, see if you can at least agree to disagree and move on.

Part Four: Teamwork Works

Support the Team

Not everyone knows how to be a team player and support the team's work. You need to be a helper. Don't be above getting your hands dirty. Team players understand that the sum of the whole is always greater than the value of the individual.

The goal in health care is to improve the quality of life and outcomes for the patients. Some nurses may be better than others at some aspects of care, while others may excel in another aspect. The expectation is not that everyone becomes a perfect nurse, but rather that each contributes what she can to the whole to provide quality care. There might be only a small, supportive role for others in some instances. In other situations, the others might play a strong leadership role, and you'll take the supportive role. Everyone pulls together to meet the goals for the unit and the patients.

You may not like every person you work with, but you should be able to respect the job they do or how they treat the patients. Some people don't have great bedside manner or people skills, but they have great compassion and can give a shot or start an IV with the least amount of pain for the patient. Or perhaps they have a great sense of humor and bring a smile to the faces of the patients.

You are going to spend a great portion of your life each day with these people. Try to find ways to build camaraderie and make the job fun and fulfilling for everyone. As time goes by, you'll develop a sense of when it's appropriate to chime in with your suggestions and as you earn the respect of your coworkers, they will begin to listen to your suggestions and appreciate them and might even ask for your input.

Part Four: Teamwork Works

Give genuinely of yourself and don't look for secondary gains. Try to get to know something about your coworkers outside of the workplace. Show an interest in who they are as people and not just as nurses or other health care workers. This will provide you with tremendous insight into how they behave in the workplace.

Leave behind your attitude of "this is how we did it in school" and open your mind to different ways of doing things. Be diplomatic. You will find your way and gain the respect of your coworkers if you are warm and friendly, honest, open to suggestion and criticism, and take responsibility for your actions.

Be open and willing to trade assignments and shifts as needed with your coworkers and you'll help to foster an atmosphere of "you scratch my back and I'll scratch yours." Show that you are a team player.

Some of your coworkers are going to see you as a threat because you represent new blood and new ideas. Others will see you as a gosling to take under their wing and mold into a similar version of themselves. Some might smother you and others can be quite helpful.

The truth is that you will learn something from everyone you work with. Try to stay focused on your own beliefs and goals and try not to get swept up in the plan for making you a clone of another nurse.

Build relationships with your coworkers. Some of them will develop into lifelong friendships as well as professional relationships. Don't be afraid to become friends with your boss, but remember that she is your boss and you need to maintain a professional relationship as well. Don't take advantage of personal friendships to gain professional stature or to promote unfair politics.

Always keep your head about you and follow your gut instincts and common sense. Some new nurses doubt their instincts when in fact most of the time they shouldn't. If a colleague advises you to do something a certain way, and you aren't comfortable about it, chances are good that it may not be right. Don't readily assume that this person is correct or that he has some hidden agenda to discredit you, but tactfully seek a second opinion. And then tactfully explain why you took a different approach if the person questions why you ignored his advice.

As you make friends and build relationships within your facility, you need to keep in mind that others will judge you by the friends you keep. You should be open and accepting of all your coworkers, but take care in choosing your close relationships.

There will be times to delegate and times not to. It's important to understand the entire situation and not to waste time and resources. The important thing to remember is who is responsible for what. Work your way backward from the person providing the direct care all the way to the physician who prescribed the care. The responsible parties also include everyone in the chain of command in the nursing realm. Where you fit into that realm, along with the extent of your personal responsibility, may differ for each of your assigned patients depending on who is assisting you in their care for that particular shift.

Delegating is a diplomatic process. You must understand the scope of practice for all involved and understand how well each person functions in his role. It is also important to understand any personal shortcomings and how well you can trust those to whom you delegate responsibilities.

If you are in charge of the unit, you are responsible for all patients and the staff under you providing their care. In this situation, you really need to know your own capabilities as well as those of your staff. You will need to implement a plan and allow yourself time to supervise all staff. In the event that you find yourselves short-staffed, you will need to call upon all your leadership abilities to ensure that everyone is working together and knows their responsibilities.

Each person needs to understand his own scope of practice and when to ask for help. It is vital to the well-being of all involved that no one oversteps his bounds, which seems to happen most often when staff members are also nursing students. Work together and listen to your coworkers. Remember, the safety and well-being of the patient is foremost. The goal is to provide quality patient care.

As an example, your best nursing assistant is in his last year of a BSN program. You're short staffed and an MD wants you to assist with a procedure now! Another patient needs to have a Foley catheter inserted because of incontinence issues and no one else can do it right now. The aide has inserted many catheters in the past month under the supervision of his instructor and feels confident. He volunteers to help you out. Don't do it! Ask the aide to explain to the patient that you have been delayed and to assist the patient by offering a bedpan or padding the bed with some waterproof pads until you can get there.

Perhaps the aide is a graduate nurse who hasn't taken boards yet—you still shouldn't take chances. An LPN may have been allowed to perform a procedure in a previous job and is willing to help out, but isn't allowed to do it here. Again, delegate responsibilities that assist you in getting to your duties quicker but that don't exceed anyone's scope of practice. On the other hand, if you're being asked to do something outside of your scope, suggest something that you can do to assist the situation, but don't take on the responsibility for something you are not allowed to do.

As a member of the health care team, your responsibility includes informing patients and their families of your role on the team. If they need more assistance than you are able to provide, help them to understand who can provide that and get the help they need. Of course, if their need is urgent, all you have to say is, "Let me get someone who can help you." Later you may have an opportunity to explain the organization to them.

Sometimes patients refer to the aide as their nurse and the RN as the treatment or medication nurse. Everyone can help alleviate this situation with a simple correction and by referring to each other by the appropriate title. The intention is to inform the patients and not to mislead them. If the patient doesn't understand your role, she may be frustrated with the care she is receiving.

Teamwork is defined as the collaborative effort of a group to achieve a common goal. In health care, the goal is to improve the quality of life and outcomes for the patient. This is achieved as all the team members involved in the patient's care work together to provide the highest possible quality of care.

Even in situations where the patient dies, if the team members have coordinated their efforts to provide the best of care and to ease the pain and suffering of the patient and his loved ones, then the effort is successful. This is an example of a situation where the expectation may not always be that the patient will get better. But it doesn't mean that even for a few seconds, the quality of the life that hung on by a thread wasn't improved just a little. Did the patient die with dignity, and were you there by his side?

Part Four: Teamwork Works

Health care naturally lends itself to teamwork. No one individual is ever solely responsible for a patient's outcomes; there will always be at least the patient and one other health care team member. More often than not, there will be several team members. Together you will work toward one goal: improving the patient's quality of life and outcomes from a spell of illness and promoting wellness.

Take time to get to know your teammates. Sometimes you will have to make the first move and other times someone will take you under her wing. In either case, if you learn a little about each person, you'll gain some insight into who your coworkers are and how they work. You won't like everyone, but if everyone is a team player, you'll be working together for a common goal, and liking or not liking won't matter much. Strive to keep up your end of the bargain and stay focused.

Teamwork always works best when everyone is a team player. As team members, you work collectively toward a common goal. If each person is working alone and for his individual stardom, you won't have a team. One person who is not a team player can spoil the effort for everyone else. This kind of person makes you want to work around him to virtually eliminate him. Sometimes that's just not possible, and the spirit of the team is broken.

The team leader or unit manager sets the tone and is responsible for keeping the team intact. All team members have to be dedicated to the common goal as well. If someone isn't working out, the entire team needs to work toward pulling her in. But the team leader is ultimately responsible to support the team in doing this. Sometimes the team has to approach the team leader and bring its concerns about this member to her attention.

59   Try Not to Leave Projects for the Next Shift

On occasion, going home at the end of your shift may not be possible. In some instances, you will be expected to stay and finish the job, and other times it might be okay to leave it for the next shift to carry on. But in all instances, your supervisor needs to know. The more advance notice you can give her, the better she can deal with the situation. Sometimes it can be delegated to someone else, and other times she can include it in the assignment for the next shift and the nurse need never know it was left over.

The biggest challenge some days will be in getting it all done without killing yourself or someone else. Some days it will seem impossible to get all your work done. Life happens. There will always be unforeseen circumstances. However, you need to strive to complete your assignment and not leave something for the next person to do.

The truth is that no one should ever be above emptying a bedpan. Your goal in becoming a nurse was to help alleviate pain and suffering and to make a difference in someone's life every day.

When you answer a call light or are just walking down the hall and get flagged down to help someone on or off a bedpan, you need to help and not put it off saying, "I'll get your aide for you." Of course, if you're on your way to another patient to assist a doctor or are right in the middle of a new admission and cannot stop, a quick explanation and a call to the aide could be appropriate. Don't overuse this excuse. Even your Director of Patient Care Services (DOPCS) or Director of Nurses (DON) has probably been seen recently rolling up her sleeves and getting back to the basics of patient care.

Part Five

The Ongoing Learning Process

Most nurses leave school and enter the work force feeling incompetent and scared to death that they don't know everything they need to know. New nurses are often struck by the lack of time they have to spend with each patient. Suddenly you are responsible for more than just the two or three patients you had as a student. Now you're expected to provide or oversee all your patients' care, not just a few hours of a shift or a few tasks to enhance your skills. The truth is you'll never know everything, and you'll continue to learn something new each day.

Learn When to Say No

As the new member of your unit, you may be compelled to volunteer every time there is a new need. This will no doubt help you to gain experience, but it can be very taxing as well. You need to know your own limitations. And you need to be mindful of what work you may be passing on to your coworkers in order to take on a new assignment.

You will be asked sometimes to work an additional shift. This shift will be either a double shift, or portion thereof, or an additional day in your workweek. You will be compensated at an overtime rate, but you should realize that overtime is taxed at a different rate and you won't be taking home a lot more money. Your primary consideration should be your ability to safely perform your duties under these circumstances and you should be honest about it with your employer before you agree.

Each unit should have a copy of the facility's policy and procedure (P&P) manual as well as a standards of care manual. Some facilities write their own manuals, others buy standard versions. Some facilities have a combination of both and cross reference to them. Be sure you know where these manuals are located and use them frequently. Make copies of pages as you use them to take home and review.

These manuals describe how a procedure is expected to be performed in this facility. Each time you perform a new procedure, you must refer to these manuals first. Even if the procedure is not new to you, if it is the first time you have performed it in this facility, you must refer to the manual. Locate your manuals and read through them. Fill any free time you have by familiarizing yourself with the contents.

Part Five: The Ongoing Learning Process

Know the "Five Rights" of Medications

There are "Five Rights" to accurate medication administration. These five rights are right medication, right dose, right time, right route, and right patient. Check the label on the bottle, bubble pack or other packaging, the doctor's order, and the medication administration record (MAR). If you are unfamiliar with this medication, check your drug book. Give the medication at the precise time. Can this medication be given as ordered? Can the patient swallow it? Or can it be crushed? Is it available in a liquid form? Verify all the above steps and then verify the patient information. Never assume that you know this patient or use the room and bed number as the sole means of identification.

Nurses learn these rules in school. The tendency to skimp on them is a problem that often stems from factors such as overconfidence and staffing shortages. There is no excuse for cutting corners; follow the rules and keep your patients safe.

Patient safety rules were made for a reason. Patient safety is one of the primary issues facing the health care industry today. It is also one of the most studied areas. According to the Institute of Medicine, approximately 98,000 Americans die each year from avoidable medical errors. One of the most prevalent reasons for medical errors is the lack of adequate information. The inability to access information is the largest challenge. Doctors and nurses don't set out to make mistakes, but if they don't have the patient's medical history at their fingertips, errors can easily be made.

Following patient safety goals and rules will help to reduce the occurrence of medical errors. Staying informed about advances in medical treatments and procedures will help as well. And encouraging your facility and coworkers to become comfortable with technological advances will help health care move more quickly into a realm where medical information is stored electronically and immediately accessible.

Part Five: The Ongoing Learning Process

Take Responsibility When an Error Occurs

Tell the truth right away. If you have done your best to follow patient safety rules and to avoid mistakes, chances are that it is a minimal mistake, but you must report it. Discuss it privately with your supervisor. Then notify the doctor and anyone else your supervisor says must be notified.

Remember the three types of errors: when you do something incorrectly; when you omit something; or when you do the wrong thing. Any one of them constitutes a reportable error. The damage done will tell you how dangerous it was, but other factors can be involved as well. These can include such things as whether you were preoccupied at the time, tried to do too many things at once, partied all night and didn't sleep well, or tried to do something by yourself and should have asked for help.

Unless you are not human, you will make a mistake once in a while. As a new nurse you will have spent countless hours feeling incompetent and stupid. You may even feel as if everything you learned in the last few years suddenly disappeared from your brain and is never coming back.

This is all perfectly normal. It's going to take time to feel confident and at ease in such situations. Every nurse before you has experienced this and they're still nurses. The chances are pretty good they didn't kill anyone.

Slow down, ask questions, and remember that no nurse ever stops learning nor will he know it all at some point.

Hopefully no one was harmed seriously. If you truly cannot figure out how it happened, you will have to let that go as well. You may understand it much later on.

An error is going to play havoc with your confidence. Expect this to happen and do all that you can to move on. If you have been keeping a journal of positive experiences, this may be the ideal time to review it and remind yourself that you have done many things in your short career to make life better for your patients. You did not intend to make this error and you will take better care never to repeat it.

Online discussion boards are full of comments from new nurses who have just made their first mistake or a colleague did and how they are dealing with it. Read them and pay attention to the responses from the experienced nurses who don't berate the new nurses and tell them they're stupid or incompetent. The experienced nurses share their own experiences, commiserate, and offer advice on how to learn from the error and put it behind you. Focus on the positive and the reasons you became a nurse. This too shall pass.

If you make a mistake, tell your supervisor right away. Take ownership of it and learn from it. What can you do to avoid it and any similar mistakes in the future? Then move on. Don't dwell on it; there is nothing more you can do.

NANDA is the acronym for the North American Nursing Diagnosis Association. This agency, which is now international, works to develop, classify, and update nursing diagnoses to help direct the nursing process.

The nursing diagnosis may be something that you use formally with written care plans and goals, or it may again be something you draw from informally. On any given day, your patients will exhibit more than one problem requiring nursing interventions.

Your goals should be patient-oriented, measurable, and realistic, such as: "The patient will state that his pain level is reduced from 9/10 to 4/10 with the use of relaxation techniques, therapeutic massage, and medication regime by day three of the current admission."

Your assessment and interventions will involve determining the signs and symptoms that contribute to the pain, finding measures that help to reduce the pain, and providing measures to both increase the patient's tolerance as well as reduce the pain.

Care Plans Keep the Team Informed

The fact is that whether or not you have a formal written plan, as you use the nursing process to deliver your care, you will formulate a care plan for each of your patients. Each time you perform a nursing intervention, you will have goals for your patient's outcomes and will assess the response to the intervention. You don't have to reinvent the wheel on each shift. Perhaps issues have been reprioritized because of some changes; the care plan disseminates this information to the team. Without some form of formal plan, the continuity of care is compromised and the quality of care and outcomes are no longer optimal.

Care plans are an important part of the health care delivery process and should be utilized. Today, as more and more unlicensed personnel are used, the level of responsibility on the RN is compounded and a road map for the care is even more essential to keeping everyone on the same page.

You need to assess all patients, diagnose their nursing health care needs, plan for their care, and implement and evaluate the care. In implementing the care plan, you always need to consider who this person is, her beliefs, and her background.

Cultural differences affect how people react to illness, how they respond to symptoms, how they seek medical care, and how they perceive the health care team members. All this affects how they will react to and respond to treatment.

You will also encounter cultural differences in your health care team. The team members will have different beliefs and strategies for handling situations and patient care issues. Nurses need to listen and be tolerant. Being understanding of differences will not only broaden your own horizons, but will also help you to become a better nurse. Ask questions, listen to the answers, be sensitive, show respect, and build trust.

Clinical Pathways Help Coordinate Patient Care

Clinical pathways are set plans for the care of a patient with a specific medical diagnosis and as such, they are not easily individualized. It is important to select a pathway that fits the most pertinent needs of the patient.

These pathways allow for expected variances but cannot possibly anticipate all combinations of factors. On the positive side, clinical pathways support continuity of care and coordinate care across the clinical disciplines by providing clinical guidelines for care. They help reduce risks and contain costs. Outcomes and documentation are usually improved significantly by the use of pathways.

Pathways are designed to standardize care and to improve the quality of care and outcomes. One of the most beneficial aspects of clinical pathways is that they include the whole team in planning and implementing care. This includes the patient, who is a major partner and player in the entire process.

You may have learned a specific technique for a procedure in school or learned that this technique replaces one commonly used for years. When you observe a nurse using a different or possibly an obsolete technique, please don't rush in with an attitude of "this is the way it should be done!" The "this is the way we did it in school" attitude is not always welcome.

As long as there are several acceptable ways of doing something, none of which poses risks for the patient, your way is what you are comfortable with and someone else's may be very different. If the patient asks, you should always explain that there are different methods to accomplish the same thing. If the patient expresses a preference, don't take offense if he doesn't choose your way, and don't make a big deal about it if he likes yours better. Respect your coworkers for their diversity.

If the other nurse is using an obsolete technique that may cause harm to the patient, calmly ask to speak to her privately and then say something like, "Maybe you haven't heard this before, but we were taught that new research says doing [that] can cause harm to the patient, and that it should be done this way." If it can wait, discuss it with the nurse privately afterward.

Part Five: The Ongoing Learning Process

With rare exceptions, most of the patients you work with will not be in a perfect state of wellness. They may have arrived at your doorstep critically injured, acutely ill, or maybe just with a few new signs and symptoms that need to be taken care of. Whatever the case, you need to always remember that your patients have a life beyond the present realm. They are mothers and fathers, sisters, brothers, grandparents, children, coworkers, and friends and family to many others you may meet.

Your patients' lives make up who they are. Their agendas that are being disrupted right now are major concerns to them. The patients may even be grieving a loss of some sort as represented by this present illness. They are also usually acutely aware of the fact that they are "not themselves" at the present moment and may not be able to cope with that either.

150 Tips and Tricks for New Nurses

Think about how you are if you have just a simple nagging headache. Your concentration is disrupted. You might be cranky and short with others around you. You don't function at your most optimal level. Someone meeting you for the first time might have a distorted view of who you are.

No one is ever at her best when she doesn't feel well. Pain, nausea, diarrhea, itching, burning, and fever all take a toll on nerves and patience. The fears of the unknown, fear of dying, and fear of pain all create a tremendous sense of discomfort. Your role as a nurse is to help the patient to retain her self-respect and dignity and to see beyond who the patient is today to who she is as a person. Help her to focus on learning how to cope and to feel confident that you will assist her to gain at least some measure of control over this situation.

Losing a Patient Is Always Difficult

Whatever your prior experience, losing a patient is never easy and conjures up a variety of emotions. Was it a sudden and unexpected event, such as an arrest in a young patient? A teenager who entered the ER via ambulance from a horrible traffic accident? After working on him for nearly an hour, your team had stabilized him, and then he suddenly arrested. Or perhaps it's an elderly woman you'd only just met yesterday, but you bonded quickly.

Each of these scenarios evokes images and emotions that represent different levels of loss and can leave you feeling inadequate or questioning your faith, just as they would if the loss had been a loved one of your own. Your patients and your profession are all part of who you are. Death will always take a personal toll.

When events evoke an emotional response, it's okay to share the moment with your patients and cry. Many things can trigger emotional reactions; most of them are sad, but happy moments can elicit tears as well.

You may encounter coworkers who don't show their emotions as part of their cultural background and personal makeup. You need to be open and accepting of cultural diversity. Likewise, they need to respect you as well. Some people see showing emotions as weak and will repress their feelings and remain controlled at all times. Sometimes, as the nurse, you may need to control your emotions to maintain control over a situation and to function normally. You may need to be strong for your patient or their loved ones. It is recommended that you allow yourself to break down and release these emotions at a later time. Like stress, emotions that are stifled for too long can be harmful both physically and mentally.

Part Five: The Ongoing Learning Process

Part Six

Communicating with Patients and Their Families

A patient's family members come in all shapes and sizes and temperaments. The most important thing you need to remember is that they will have their own set of issues and coping mechanisms related to the patient's illness as well. A lot of times, family members will be your best allies in dealing with and helping the patient. They are often the primary caregivers. They know the patient best and can interpret and translate why the patient is having a certain reaction or isn't coping with a situation.

76 Discharge Planning Starts at Admission

At the moment a patient is admitted, the clock starts ticking down the time that the payer allots for this spell of illness. Patients and families may have no idea that the patient won't remain in that bed until he is completely well, or even able to care for himself again. They need to be educated, and they need to understand that the patient's stay will be short.

You will learn the patterns of how long certain payers will allow a patient to stay, and you will always be begged by some patients or their loved ones to do what you can to help them stay just a little longer. There will be little to nothing that you can do except to instruct them to discuss it with the physician and discharge planner or case manager.

One of the most useful and effective aspects of communication is listening. Communication is a two-way process: listening and speaking. However, communication is not effective unless you listen as well as speak, and you listen well. Many times the person just wants someone to listen—not even to respond, just to listen.

When you listen to what someone else has to say, you show respect and validate her right to her feelings. Sometimes people just need to hear themselves say something out loud in order to better understand it themselves. Sometimes they just want someone to listen to them vent. And sometimes they need you to listen and to help them sort out their feelings and find solutions. Listen to family members, and then ask what you can do to help. Be sure to enlist their help in fixing the situation.

Keep the Family Informed

Many times problems can be avoided by anticipating needs and keeping patients and family members informed. Give them an approximate schedule of the day's events. If a family member wants to speak with the physician, let the person know what time the doctors typically make rounds. This is usually in the early morning and could be well worth the family member missing a few hours of work to get some important information. If this isn't possible, encourage the person to speak to the doctor's nurse and find out when he typically returns phone calls. Many times, physicians return nonemergency calls after hours.

In most cases, you'll defuse a lot of explosive situations just by listening and validating the person's right to be upset or afraid. Let him know that you are there to help and that you are on his side. Empower him by making him part of the team and giving him some responsibility.

The fact is that your patients are an important part of your life. There will be some who touch your life more than others. You will play an important role in their lives. It is only natural that you will develop attachments and share their feelings of elation when things work out and go well. So you will also share in their disappointment and sadness when things go wrong.

Students either dearly love or detest their clinical rotations in labor and delivery because they tend to become so emotional when participating in the birth process. And some nurses find that hospice is the most rewarding niche of all for them because they feel hospice is where they can make the biggest difference in someone's life. Others just can't handle the constant issues of death and dying. Caring is what you do best, so you just have to find the niche where you can do it best.

Part Six: Communicating with Patients and Their Families

Anyone facing a change in day-to-day life will experience a grief process. Illness presents a change. How dramatic that change is depends on the intensity of the illness. Your patient will run through the stages of grief as he deals with the onset of symptoms, receives the diagnosis, and learns to cope with the treatment and gets back to a new point of wellness.

Remember the stages of grief as described by Elisabeth Kübler-Ross, MD. They are the following: denial, anger, bargaining, depression, and acceptance. The intensity and duration of each stage will depend largely on the significance of the change or loss. And remember, these stages are not always experienced in order and some may be skipped altogether. Anger, depression, and denial are usually the most obvious behaviors demonstrated and should be your most obvious clues to issues with coping.

You'll find yourself from time to time in an uncomfortable place—in the middle of family arguments and disagreements about a patient's care. There may be very good, sound, even reasonable reasons for not telling the patient something, but that may not be the best thing for the patient. Remember that you are not alone in this situation. Nurses enjoy a lot of autonomy and independence in their roles, but this is not the ideal situation for working alone.

Nurses have a tendency to try to handle situations on their own. But you must remember that health care is a team activity. Besides you and the patient, the physician is also a primary team member. The team also includes your supervisor and the facility you work for, as well as coworkers and multidisciplinary team members who would be involved in this patient's care.

Honor the Family's Wishes

When the family doesn't want the patient to know about her prognosis, you need to listen to the family members and gather as much information about why they think this is a good idea. Perhaps they will convince you and perhaps you can gently persuade them to consider the fact that the patient has a right to know. At least until the doctor is involved, you need to respect their wishes.

Next, you need to gather information from the patient about what she understands to be her diagnosis and what she understands about the things the doctor has told her. This might be difficult to do if the family hovers constantly, but you need to try. Sometimes the patient is very much aware and knows that her family doesn't want her to know, so she plays along with it. If that's the case, you just need to be sure to let the rest of the team know what's going on.

When the patient doesn't want the family to know about his illness, this can also be an uncomfortable situation, but patients have a right to privacy. In fact, with HIPAA rules, you pretty much have to act as if the patient has made this request unless you have his authorization to do otherwise.

As with any portion of the patient's care, if his privacy issues are adversely affecting his care or condition, you need to discuss this with the patient and the rest of the team. Discharge planning begins at admission. If his safety is going to be compromised because of secrecy, then the situation needs to be discussed as a component to his care.

You have the responsibility to honor his requests for privacy, but you also have the responsibility to ensure that he understands the possible consequences. You have to make him responsible for his own health status and to advocate for his wellness.

Part Six: Communicating with Patients and Their Families

Take the Time to Educate Your Patients

Each time you encounter your patient, you're assessing her and the situation. You're also carrying out the planned care and evaluating its necessity and success or failure. The data you gather is both subjective and objective. Listen to what your patient tells you. What has she learned about her experience? What does she understand about her signs and symptoms? What does she know about how to control them?

Each time you give a medication to your patients, you should tell them what it is and what it's for. If they already know this, then ask them something about the medication or the diagnosis for which they are taking the medication.

Every encounter with your patients is a learning experience for them. Recognize the opportunity and make the most of it. Each effort you make will help to improve the outcomes and help your patients to become accountable for their own health care status.

Teaching your patients about their health status—how to cope, what to expect, and what to do in certain situations—empowers them. It involves them in their care and gives them responsibilities for their own outcomes. It makes them self-reliant and independent, even if they still need some assistance. You can help patients understand their role and responsibility in their own health status. They are the directors.

So many people believe that when they have an ailment and the doctor gives them a pill, they get better. They don't always understand the impact of their lifestyle and other risk factors. Health education falls on the nurse. More and more, as health care costs rise, nurses are finding they need to fill this role. If health care costs are ever going to be contained, consumers need to take responsibility to understand their health status and to improve it using all measures possible.

Part Six: Communicating with Patients and Their Families

Combine Visual Demonstrations with Verbal Instructions

Some people will learn best from your verbal explanations, while others require a demonstration or pictures. Some can follow step-by-step instructions well, while others need to see the finished product before they can learn the steps. Some learn best by doing things themselves, while others retain the information better by watching several times first. Ask your patient what works best for him. How does he learn how to do things at work, at home, or with hobbies? By the same token, some nurses are better at teaching by telling and others by showing. Think about what your strengths are, and if your patient needs something different, ask a coworker to try another approach.

Return demonstration is a vital part of patient teaching. Never assume that a patient understands and is competent without having him demonstrate it to you. And always document what has been taught, verbalized back, and return demonstrated, as well as what needs to be reviewed.

Look at the whole patient, not just the disease. How many times was this drummed into your head in school? By now, you should have a good understanding of this concept. In order to individualize the care plan and maximize the outcomes for each patient, you have to look at the whole patient. Enlist the patient and his family and caregivers to see beyond the diagnosis as well. You need to help your patients, their families, and caregivers to understand that all the patient's personal habits and lifestyle choices will need to be incorporated into long-term plans for coping with his health status. The patient's family, job, hobbies, culture, diet, and habits all contribute to his illness and risk factors. Some patients won't share these with you, and you will need to help them understand that they need to examine them for themselves in order to promote wellness and improve their outcomes.

Part Six: Communicating with Patients and Their Families

Beware of Misinformation

One of the dangers of the prevalence of television and other advertising media pushing drugs is misinformation. It is one thing if the drug is a prescription, and quite another if it's an over-the-counter (OTC) remedy. However, it can sometimes be quite easy to get a physician to write that prescription without a thorough diagnostic process.

So many people believe that if they read something in a reputable periodical or see it on TV, it must be true. While these advertisements are generally truthful, the general public doesn't hold medical or pharmacological degrees. Patients might have a couple of the vague symptoms and think this new medicine will cure what ails them. If one brand of cold medicine didn't work, they'll try another (which most likely contains the same ingredients). Worse yet, if one dose didn't work, then they think that maybe a double dose will, and they may unknowingly overdose.

Asking what the patient knows or what he has understood to be said is always an effective teaching strategy. This may provide clues to his understanding of anatomy and physiology as well as disease and treatment modalities and options. A diagnosis of cancer often comes with big misconceptions. To some, it is a death sentence no matter what type and site. Many men also have the strange misconception that having a vasectomy will leave them impotent or at the very least cause some erectile dysfunction.

You need to know where the gaps are and what information the patient needs to fill them in. If you are authorized to discuss the patient's care with family members, you again need to understand their knowledge base and deficits, what they have learned from the doctor and the patient, and what else they need to know.

Part Six: Communicating with Patients and Their Families

Involve the Family in Discharge Planning

To maximize patient/family/caregiver education and improve discharge planning, routines may need to be reconsidered. Explore options for ensuring family members/caregivers are present. This includes having the caregiver come in early or delaying the procedure until the family member can be present. It also requires coordination of care with several parties including staff, the patient, and the family members.

Since the advent of shorter hospital stays, patients are being discharged much sicker than may be ideal and in need of much more complex and technologically challenging care. They may or may not qualify for, or have coverage for, home health services. Family members and other caregivers may be expected to assume full and immediate responsibility for assisting patients with this care.

Daily procedures may need to be switched to a later time frame in order to accommodate family members and to facilitate their instruction in the care. One reason that home care nurses complain about poor teaching in the hospital is that daily procedures may be routinely done in the early morning and not during visiting hours or times when family members can be present. Consequently, patients are discharged with inadequate preparation.

If you are dispensing a new medication, instruct the patient in its name, action, dose, and any side effects or other implications. For instance, if your patient has just started taking an anticoagulant medication, instruct him in bleeding precautions and measures to reduce injuries. Discuss the reason for this medication such as a recent thrombosis or CVA, or as a prophylactic measure following joint replacement surgery.

If the patient needs assistance to get out of bed to go to the bathroom and back, instruct the caregiver in proper body mechanics and transfer techniques. Encourage the caregiver to participate in the lessons to learn how to safely manage the patient. Demonstrate the use of a gait belt or other measures to assist with safe ambulation. Correct any bad habits and work to instill confidence that they can do this in both the patient and his caregiver.

Encourage other staff to instruct the patients in their responsibilities for care as well. If the patient is going to need assistance with activities of daily living (ADLs) at home, have the family member present for meals, bathing, bed making, etc., to learn tips and tricks to help make their job easier once the patient is home.

Part Six: Communicating with Patients and Their Families

Part Seven

Communication with Doctors

Physicians can be intimidating just because of their vast knowledge and education. New nurses especially can fall prey to this. What you always need to remember is to put the respective roles into perspective. Your role is just as vital to the patient, but in a different way. Respect the physician's knowledge and tap into it as often as you can. But know that it doesn't make him a better person or more of a professional than you.

Doctors Just Want the Facts

In all instances, the physician must be kept apprised of the patient's condition. The one thing to keep in mind in communicating with physicians is that they are busy and almost always just want the facts. They will want a specific picture of the situation. Never call the doctor when you don't have a recent set of vital signs and an assessment to provide. Always have your facts in front of you, and not where you have to dig to find them. Make notes and compose your thoughts. Listen to their orders, read them back, and ask for verification of what you read back. Be concise, accurate, honest, and up front. If you are unfamiliar with something, say so, and ask for a simple explanation or clarification. Identify yourself and state your credentials (RN or LVN). If communicating by phone, clearly identify where you are calling from and which patient you are calling about.

Nurses have evolved as professionals and have firmly established their own essential roles in health care. They complement the physician's care, but both are vital, primary members of the health care team. The nurse-doctor relationship has evolved along with nursing roles. Respect physicians and expect them to respect you.

As gender becomes less of an issue for both nurses and doctors, both professions have grown in respect for each other. Realizing that each is a profession and not a gender has opened many avenues of communication and respect. New doctors and nurses have brought to their respective professions a new sense of teamwork and camaraderie that has broken down a number of barriers and achieved a more equal relationship.

Doctors and nurses have very different jobs, and each of them is equally important to the patient's health care issues. Neither is superior or inferior to the other. Doctors and nurses deserve to be treated with respect and dignity.

Part Seven: Communication with Doctors

Earn the Doctors' Trust

As a new nurse, introduce yourself to the physicians. As with any of your team members, smile, use direct eye contact, and shake their hands. Make a positive first impression. Let them know that you look forward to working with them. Take the time to get to know them and to build a rapport. Ask appropriate questions, and let them teach you. Most doctors love to teach.

Show them that they can trust you and that you will provide the care they expect for their patients. This will go a long way in the event that you have a question about an order, or when there has been an error. They will usually make the extra effort to explain, teach, or clarify something without an attitude of indignation. And though they may be angry or disappointed if there is an error, they will understand that you are human and will do the right thing to correct it.

Physicians have tremendous responsibilities for the well-being of their patients. Time constraints and financial issues contribute to these responsibilities as well. For far too long, the general public has viewed doctors as being god-like or having powers to perform miracles. Physicians fostered this by allowing their egos to expand to enormous levels. In the past, physicians had an attitude of superiority unequaled by almost any other profession. Sometimes a physician's bedside manner was atrocious, and his treatment of other health care professionals was unacceptable.

As nurses demand respect and refuse to be doormats, physicians have had to evolve as well. There still are and will continue to be some who have the "God complex." The number of these types of doctors will shrink as time goes on. In general, nurses avoid these doctors as much as possible; they learn how to stay out of their way, and word spreads throughout the ranks.

Handle Egos with Care

You may have a hard time dealing with some doctors. For some, you may have to stroke their egos a bit. Depending on the person, as long as they get their attention and feel superior, they'll be nice (and you can make faces at them behind their backs the whole time). Anticipate what they want from you. Get their patients' needs attended to and send them off to their office as soon as possible.

If you question an order, remember that doctors are human and can make mistakes. They could also have good reason for something. If you use an approach such as, "I've never seen that dose for that medication; could you please explain why such a high dose is necessary for this patient?" you're more likely to get a nice answer than if you put them on the spot and say, "That's not the normal dose."

Always remember to act as part of a team, especially in front of your patients. No matter how difficult it may be to work with some people, remember that your goals are the same—helping a patient be healthy.

Health care is very a consumer-driven field these days, with all the managed care efforts, and physicians have had to learn to play the game. Patients have been forced to change physicians because of insurance coverage requirements, and as a result, patients also have new feelings of empowerment: if they don't like their doctor, they can change. People used to be afraid of hurting the doctor's feelings. Others never knew that doctors could be caring souls. Now, if they don't like their doctor's attitude, they move on.

Care facilities have also found that they have the right to make choices, and, for instance, some home health agencies refuse to take patients from physicians who are considered abusive to the staff. In all honesty, they may not have a staff member willing and able to take on that case. The agencies stand behind their staff and will not expose them to this abuse any more than they will to any other unsafe situation.

97   Remain Professional at All Times

Nurses do need to advocate for their patients, but they also need to be professional and careful not to influence them. If you have a patient whose physician is difficult to work with, you need to follow his orders and care for his patient the same as any other. You can't express your opinion to the patient or family members. You need to be professional and keep it to yourself. If they bring it up, the only comment you could make is to remind them that they have choices and leave it at that.

Patients may ask you to recommend a physician, but you should not do so. You can provide them with the names of several doctors to choose from, but you need to remain unbiased. Your facility may have rules that forbid making such recommendations, and in that case you must tell the patients to call a physician referral service or other resource.

Violence in the workplace includes verbal abuse and threats. Employers can be liable for not protecting employees from this kind of behavior. Nurses for far too long were subservient to doctors, but that has changed, and abuse is not tolerated any longer. Health care facilities often placed a greater value on the revenue these physicians bring in than on the value of their employees. Those facilities that still adhere to this practice open themselves not only to liability issues, but also to tremendous problems with retention of staff. Many hospitals have instituted policies and rules that require physicians to attend classes on how to treat nurses and other health care staff and professionals.

Part Seven: Communication with Doctors

Stand Up for Yourself

Some doctors are notorious for having tempers and throwing tantrums. You will most likely be a witness or be subjected to one of these, sooner or later. If you were wrong, say so. Be honest and up front at all times. If you say something like, "You have every right to be angry. I would be furious too," you'll defuse the situation somewhat. Let the doctor vent. If you weren't in error, say so.

Never make a scene in front of the patient. If the physician chooses to demonstrate her unprofessional behavior in such a manner, let her. You should have more respect for yourself and your patients than that. Ask to speak to her privately later and let her know that she was rude or inappropriate. Even if you were wrong, she has no right to reprimand you in front of the patients and your peers. You are entitled to privacy for this kind of conversation.

Almost every physician has a love of teaching. Some are better at it than others, but take advantage of every opportunity that you can to broaden your knowledge base. Establish a rapport with the physicians, and they will respect you and even seek you out to teach you. You also need to be astute and understand when the physician is rushed or the time is not right. These are informal mentoring situations. Don't push, and don't take it personally if the doctor does not welcome the opportunity at a particular moment.

Remember that not all physicians are cold and uncaring; rather, most of them are very compassionate and helpful. They may appear to be aloof sometimes in order to set limits and to be able to attend to all their patients. But usually they want to help you to be better able to help their patients.

Be a Good Student

Be prepared and ask appropriate questions. Do your homework. When a physician has instructed you on a topic, do a little research to expand on what she has taught you. If you work in a teaching hospital, try to make occasional rounds with the interns, especially if this physician is teaching. If not, ask to accompany the physician as she makes her rounds of your unit. Share your knowledge with your coworkers so that they will be happy to cover your patients for a few minutes.

If you find information about a subject you have discussed with your mentors, share it with them and ask for their input. Perhaps it's something new that they haven't read yet, or maybe it's just additional information and they can fill in the gaps for you.

You will undoubtedly hear some wild tales and sometimes even horror stories about some of the physicians. Some prefer a dressing to be done a certain way, some don't want faxes sent to their offices, and some want a head-to-toe assessment with every phone call you make to them. Some expect all their ordered labs to be done STAT (from statim, a Latin term meaning "immediately") and reported to them within the hour.

Doctors' quirks and demands are part of the unwritten rules of the game, and in many cases, learning these as quickly as possible will benefit you. You need to remain open-minded and form your own opinions. You also need to heed the unwritten rule of being discreet when discussing individuals. Listen to your coworkers and heed their advice, but learn to keep your opinions to yourself and always be professional. Show respect for others, and they will respect you.

Part Seven: Communication with Doctors

The first rule about dating coworkers is to be sure to understand the rules of your facility regarding this matter, including the unwritten ones, before you get involved with anyone. Dating a coworker can be a precarious situation in any profession or workplace. Sometimes these relationships work out, and many marry and live long happy lives together; other times, these relationships can be short-lived and messy. To avoid these kinds of situations, some employers forbid any type of fraternization with coworkers other than group social gatherings.

If your facility doesn't forbid dating coworkers, proceed with great caution. If it doesn't work out, you may need to change jobs in order to avoid the uncomfortable situation you have made for yourself. When people break up, their friends often have to choose whose side to be on. When you all have to work together, this may be a big challenge.

If you are dating a doctor or someone else in a more powerful position within the facility, you will most likely be seen to be brown nosing. Any advancement or promotions you might receive will probably be seen as special favors and not something you earned. Keep that in mind.

Dating a coworker can create distractions as well. You might find yourself spending a great deal of time trying to steal moments to be together and alone or to discuss plans that could wait for after hours. If you are fighting or unhappy with each other, you can find yourselves being inappropriate to each other. Dating coworkers can also put you in a competition with others who may have shared a relationship with this person before, or someone who is jealous of your relationship. If you're going to date a physician or other coworker, keep these points in mind:

- Understand your facility's rules first.
- Be discreet at all times and avoid public displays of affection.
- Never disclose private or intimate details of your relationship or about your partner to your coworkers.

- Don't spend all your free time at work (breaks and meals) with your partner.
- Don't take your problems to work with you. Leave your disagreements at home. Be professional.

Never get caught up in gossip and rumors about coworkers. Be discreet and stay out of other people's business. For instance, imagine that a doctor and your nursing supervisor were seen having dinner one night in an intimate restaurant. The rumors began flying early the next morning. People had suspected something for a while, but now there had been an actual sighting. The doctor is married. He's also angling for a position on the hospital board. A public affair could spell real trouble for him. Now imagine how embarrassed everyone was to find out that your nursing supervisor is his sister-in-law, and they were planning a surprise party for his wife's fortieth birthday!

To some, Dr. Heart may seem to be an angry old woman who hates nurses and makes unreasonable demands. Perhaps she reminds you of your favorite great aunt who is crotchety and demanding. You recognize the same odd sense of humor and understand that this woman sets the bar high. She demands excellence and wants her patients' needs met without asking. She's quick and to the point, wastes no time, and expects that nurses be prepared and anticipate her needs. Your coworkers will marvel that you get along with this woman!

Others may think that Dr. Jones is a terrific doctor because he's charming and so good-looking. His bedside manner is great, but you've seen better doctors. He is too concerned with making everyone like him to set limits and to expect his patients to do a little more for themselves. The nurses all seem to dote on his every request, but you see through his façade.

No matter what you might think on your first meeting with a doctor (or anyone, for that matter), consider that this person may have many levels and try to get to know him/her before your attach an opinion. You do have to work with this person, remember—try to give him/her the benefit of the doubt!

Part Seven: Communication with Doctors

Part Eight

Take Care of Yourself

Health care is a stressful job and is not always conducive to the best nutrition, elimination, and rest and relaxation habits. Are you taking your breaks and meals or are you routinely skipping them? Do you get to the bathroom regularly or are you holding it for hours at a time? All these factors can affect your own health issues

Hospitals are notoriously good places for harboring and transmitting germs. Other health care settings can be just as dangerous to your health. Your day-to-day exposure to patients with a variety of airborne bacteria and germs makes you susceptible. Even with the best hand-washing and infection control habits, you are bound to catch something.

Any underlying conditions you may have can become worse in such environments. If you have any autoimmune diseases such as diabetes or multiple sclerosis, you may find them out of control or out of remission. You may need to take steps to ensure that you eat properly and get enough rest. If you have respiratory problems such as asthma, you may be prone to catching a cold every time someone is admitted with a full-blown respiratory illness or even a simple case of the sniffles.

Hand-washing is the most effective form of infection control and a standard precaution. You need to wash your hands before and after contact with each patient. You also need to wash your hands between the dirty and clean aspects of procedures such as dressing changes. If you touch your mouth or your hair, you need to wash again. If you handle equipment or trash, you need to wash your hands.

Every door handle and bed rail you touch will harbor germs. And, of course, after you visit the bathroom, you must wash your hands. This not only helps to stop the spread of infections and bacteria between patients, but also helps to eliminate you from becoming contaminated and getting sick. If you contaminate a surface, you need to follow your facility's protocols for cleaning it. This is often done with a diluted bleach solution.

Part Eight: Take Care of Yourself

Build Up Your Body's Defenses

Some of the commonsense things you can do to ward off problems include talking to your physician (or other qualified person such as a nutritionist) about vitamins and minerals that may help to boost your immunity. You need to drink plenty of fluids and eat well-balanced meals at regular intervals. You also need to make sure you get plenty of rest. This may seem impossible with your new work schedule, but you need to do what you can to maximize the effort.

In many instances, you will adjust to the new environment and in time find that you are not as prone to catching things as you once were. You will build up an immunity to the germs that reside in or frequent your facility.

Don't forget to teach your patients proper hygiene, such as covering their mouths and noses when they cough or sneeze. Teach them to place their tissues in a bedside trash bag instead of leaving them all over the bed. Teach them to wash their hands when they cough or sneeze and to use the tissue.

Encourage patients to have a bedside waterless hand sanitizer available if they can't get out of bed easily or if they cough or sneeze frequently. Instruct them to take this precaution at home as well to avoid infecting family members or reinfecting themselves. If you work diligently to eliminate the germs that you can be exposed to, you will reduce your own chances of catching something.

It's normal to get caught up in the efforts to protect patients from nosocomial infections and other hospital- or facility-borne illness, but it is equally as important to remember that you are also protecting yourself from the spread of disease.

Stress can cause headaches and lead to migraines, backaches, and digestive problems such as constipation and diarrhea. Stress causes ulcers and can lead to heart attacks and strokes. Stress will exacerbate any underlying disease you might have such as diabetes or hypertension.

In the course of having to take control of situations all day long at work, nurses often turn into "control freaks" who want to have the last say in everything. The truth is that no one can be in charge of every situation, and the trick is to figure out how to not stress over everything that you cannot control. You need to learn to act and not to react to situations. The first step is to accept that you are not in control of every situation. Some situations you can contribute to and others you will just have to leave up to others to control.

When your life is always running full-speed ahead, it can be difficult to ascertain what is significant and what isn't—everything seems to be dramatic. Slow down, and let life come into perspective. Take control of your life, and manage your stress. Sleep, nutrition, and exercise are key elements to controlling your stress. You need to balance them in your life. And you need to learn to relax. You should take some time each day to unwind. Your body needs to rest and recover. Set aside time and make it a priority in your life to just shut down for a few minutes.

You need to remember not to sweat the insignificant things. Take a deep breath and consider whether this is a big enough issue to worry about. If not, let go of it. If it is a significant issue, then calming down will help you find appropriate solutions.

Part Eight: Take Care of Yourself

Practice Relaxation

Relaxation may not come naturally to you, especially if you're on a constant adrenalin high. Start with deep breathing. Sit in a comfortable position. Inhale through your nose and exhale through your mouth. Do this slowly and rhythmically. Close your eyes and imagine you are in your favorite place, all warm and snug and secure. Tense your whole body, and as you continue breathing, slowly relax your toes, then your lower legs, then your lower torso, then your upper torso, then your neck, and finally your facial muscles and your entire head. Continue breathing slowly. If you aren't completely relaxed, repeat the tensing and releasing. You can isolate areas such as your shoulders, neck, and head to relax if you need to. Devote ten to fifteen minutes to this every day, and you will begin to see results within a week or two, if not immediately.

Nursing has the highest risk for back injuries of any profession. You must do everything possible to protect your back. Most of these injuries are preventable. Stop and think before you do something that may injure yourself. Assess the situation and get help! Never try to move a patient by yourself. You could end your hands-on nursing career with one wrong move.

Proper body mechanics are essential in transferring and moving patients to sitting positions in bed. Hospital beds and tables are usually on wheels, but they have safety locks. Be sure to unlock them first. Also consider the additional weight of the patient to the weight of the bed before attempting to move it. Never skip any steps even if the patient is a small child. One wrong move can cost you your job and your back. Use gait belts and draw sheets whenever possible. And always get help from another team member.

Follow these rules when lifting or transferring patients to protect your back:

- Keep your lower back in its normal curved or arched position at all times.
- Move as close to the bed or patient as you can.
- Never twist; always pivot or side step.

- When lifting, set your feet in a position to give yourself a solid, wide base of support.
- Keep your stomach muscles tight, bow slightly at the hips, and then squat.
- Keep your head up and hold your shoulders upright. If you held a yardstick along your back, it would be perfectly straight.
- Push up from your knees and use your own momentum to help you lift.

If you do get hurt, report it right away and seek medical treatment. Early intervention is the key to successful treatment and prevention of permanent dysfunction. The trend now is to combine anti-inflammatory medications with physical therapy and as much normal activity as can be tolerated. Cumulative damage to your back can result in a very minor injury becoming the final straw that triggers a serious situation. Take care and seek treatment even for minor injuries.

The various needleless systems virtually eliminate the needle stick problem from IVs. Other forms of needle safety for hypodermic needles have been adopted across the country as well. These include needle guards that fold over the needle and syringes that allow the needle to be retracted after use. These systems help to reduce needle sticks from sharps containers by adding another barrier, but the sharps container should never be overfilled.

Always employ safeguards to protect yourself from a needle stick. Never recap and always have a sharps container within reach to dispose of the syringe and needle immediately after injection.

In the unlikely event of a needle stick, you must report it immediately. You need to be tested for exposure to such diseases as HIV and hepatitis B and C. Precautions need to be taken and possible future care needs to be ensured. Don't put yourself and your rights at risk by hiding the event.

Part Eight: Take Care of Yourself

Use Your Sick Days

If you are truly sick, stay home. Don't bring your germs to work; your coworkers and your patients really don't want to share your germs. See your doctor if necessary. Get rest and drink fluids so that you can get well as soon as possible. In an already short-staffed environment, they need you back at work.

Don't try to overextend yourself. Some nurses work three twelve-hour shifts a week at one hospital and two or three shifts at another. This may make you a lot of money, but it can wear you down and burn you out quickly. Be reasonable and realistic. Sooner or later those who overextend themselves hit a brick wall. That's when mistakes and injuries are more likely to happen. Take care of yourself, and if you are sick, keep your germs at home.

It is not up to your employer to ensure that you take your breaks—it is up to you. Make sure you take your breaks. It's easy to get into the habit of skipping them and in some units, to feel like you can't take a break because it's so busy and you are so short-staffed. You may experience peer pressure to skip breaks.

Even if you can't take the full amount of time because you are so busy, try to take some time. You do need to eat and to take bathroom breaks. Help each other to be able to do so. This is where a strong team approach will be most helpful. Don't abuse the situation, but do help each other to get away from the unit. Some facilities have breakers or float personnel who just cover for breaks and meals. A unit must have a licensed person on duty at all times.

Part Eight: Take Care of Yourself

Take a Break to Prevent Burnout

While recent studies have not shown that nurses who don't get breaks make more errors than those who do, the studies have also shown that among nurses who do take breaks, those with longer ones are less prone to making mistakes. The findings also show that staff burnout and staff departure are major problems related to not getting breaks. What this most likely means is that nurses who aren't taking breaks are intensely aware of the potential for harm; they are making more of an effort to protect their patients as well as their licenses. This added stress will eventually lead to burnout and cause nurses to leave their position.

You really need to be able to walk away from the job for a few minutes and clear your head. This will help to relieve stress and to give you a new perspective on the tasks at hand.

150 Tips and Tricks for New Nurses

You need to create your own rewards. Pat yourself on the back for finally mastering a skill or technique. Recognize that you have gone the extra mile to make a difference today. Rewarding yourself with items such as a new uniform, shoes, stethoscope, and even a special pen can bring a renewed sense of excitement about going to work for a while.

Don't forget to reward yourself just for doing a job well. Have a massage or a spa treatment. Buy those tickets to the theater or concert; you're worth it! Take time to read or enjoy a hobby, and don't feel guilty about letting the laundry pile up another day. Sleep in on your day off and enjoy a day of leisure once in a while. Take time to truly smell the roses. Surround yourself with the little things you love and that hold meaning and are important to you.

There are a number of formal stress relief measures such as meditation, imagery, breathing exercises, and relaxation techniques to help you de-stress. Join a club or group activity to explore a similar interest such as scrap-booking or creative writing. Play on an adults' sports team. Take those tennis lessons or piano lessons you gave up years ago. Address your spiritual needs.

Find support systems. The knowledge that you are not alone in your feelings needs to be reinforced from time to time. You need feedback to help ensure that you are well centered. Coworkers and friends from school are often excellent choices for some of your support systems because they share common issues. You can vent, and they will have the best understanding of what you are going through. Family and friends are great support systems as well. Support systems will help to recharge your emotional and spiritual energy.

Nurses can be the worst patients and their own worst enemies when it comes to their health status. It's usually easier to tell someone else how and what to do than it is to do it yourself, but nurses need to take care of themselves. With all the added mental and physical job-related stress taking a toll on their bodies, maintaining wellness is an important issue.

Just as you instruct your patients, you need to schedule routine exams and not skip appointments. It's not always easy to schedule them around work, but if you make a concerted effort, sometimes you can squeeze a couple of appointments into one day. Get your checkups and see the doctor if you're sick. It's important to have a physical once a year and to have a Pap smear and mammogram or prostate examination. You also need to see your dentist and have your teeth cleaned every six months.

Part Nine

Staying on Top of Documentation

Your documentation reflects the care you have or have not provided to your patient and is your only legal proof that you did or did not do something. Your documentation needs to be as important as the care you provide. Often, nurses feel that the hands-on care is all that is important and that the documentation is a waste of time. This is never the case. These responsibilities should carry equal importance at all times, because your documentation becomes a part of the patient's medical record.

Good Writing Skills Are Essential

The skill with which you write about your assessment, intervention, and the patients' outcomes will reflect on the quality of the hands-on care you provide. Your records must be clear, concise, complete, and accurate. Other health care providers will rely on this information to make decisions about the patient's care and needs.

Your writing skills need to be proficient enough to provide a reflection of your observations, which will include your assessment, your identification of problems and issues, your plan and interventions, and an evaluation of the outcomes. Terms need to be specific and factual, not vague and nondescript.

It is important to remember that the health care record is a legal document and that documentation is not optional. Nor is it trivial and unimportant. The cliché about no job being done until the paperwork is completed is perhaps more true of health care than almost any other profession.

After you have completed a few tasks, take a moment to chart. Be sure to include all pertinent data regarding patient complaints such as pain or nausea, how well a patient tolerated a procedure, the size of wounds, the color of any drainage, odors, and signs and symptoms of infection or healing. If you did any patient or family teaching, document the outcome and note what they need to do or learn next.

If you document as you go along, you'll find yourself ready to go home at the end of the day without having to spend another hour doing paperwork. Things will be fresh in your mind, and you'll be far less likely to forget some all-important information than if you let the day get away from you. If you do forget something, be sure that you know how to add an addendum to your notes and how to document an event out of order.

Accuracy is essential. If you don't have a measuring device, you'd better get one immediately. For now, give approximations or compare to the size of something similar such as a quarter or fifty-cent-piece and state that they are approximations. Next time, be sure to measure accurately.

Timeliness of your documentation is also important. You want to document as soon as you can so that the event is fresh in your mind and you don't forget important aspects. Even with careful notes, if you wait until the end of the shift to do all your documentation, you may find yourself rushing to finish and even mixing up your patients' data.

Never document ahead of time. Also, be honest and don't document something you didn't do or didn't observe yourself. You can state that someone else (and identify them) stated that some event occurred with such and such outcome, but don't say it was your observation when it was not.

Information does no good if it's all stored in your head. You might be able to accurately document each of your patients at the end of the shift, but what happens if you leave the floor for a break or a meal and haven't done any documentation? If something happens with any of your patients, the first place others are going to look for clues is in the chart. Beyond that, they're going to hunt down the person who is covering for you.

Any time you leave the unit for any reason, you need to report off to someone. That will usually be your supervisor, but you should also report off to anyone who is going to keep an eye on your patients for you. Whenever possible, you should have your documentation up-to-date before you leave. That may not always be possible, so a verbal report is essential.

Record Everything in Writing

The medical record is your proof that you did or did not do something. Always document as soon as possible especially when administering medications and treatments. Remember to include accurate information regarding site, route, and the patient's response or outcome. If the patient refuses a medication or treatment, be sure to record this information and that you have notified the doctor.

You can go back and amend your documentation at any time as long as you can honestly state that you remember the event. You must clearly state that this is an amendment and include the time and date that you are amending the record. If you are changing a statement because it is erroneous, you can mark through it, initial it, and reference where to find the amendment. Make sure that the information being corrected is still legible. And again make note in your amendment of the time and date of the new entry.

If you forgot to do something, it is as much an error as if you did the wrong thing. You need to report omissions and to complete any incident reports or other documentation required by your facility. As with any other error or incident, you must always be honest and up front about the situation. Never try to cover it up. And don't be a tattletale and run to your supervisor about someone else's omission error. Bring it to the private attention of the individual and let her handle it: If she doesn't, then privately speak to your supervisor about your concerns.

If the omission is one of forgetting to document something and no repercussions have followed, then you can amend your documentation as previously discussed. However, if events occurred as a result, such as Mr. Jones having to have an extra set of enemas, then you must also notify the doctor and complete any required incident forms.

Medical Records Are Legal Documents

Remember that the medical record is a legal document. It must be factual and accurate. You want to be precise, concise, clear, and comprehensive. You may record your observations but not your interpretations. You may also quote the patient, but be careful not to use anything out of context. Always follow these tips, and your documentation will be an asset to the care you provide: Be accurate and honest; document in a timely manner—only during or after providing the care; provide complete information regarding assessment, nursing diagnosis, nursing interventions and the plan of care, and evaluation of outcomes; be sure it is legible and in permanent ink; and be sure all information needed for any forms used is complete and accurate.

Never chart ahead of time. Don't document something until you have actually done it, and when you document it, be accurate in your time frames. Erroneous documentation can have the same ramifications as other errors.

If a wound is ugly and disgusting, saying so no doubt conveys a message, but does not accurately describe the wound. The following gives a much clearer description of the wound: "The old dressing was removed. The R hip wound is now 3 cm. by 4 cm. by 0.5 cm. There is 1 cm. strip of yellow slough along the entire right side that is well adhered. There is pink granulation tissue around the outer edges of the other three sides. There is a slight odor emanating from the slough, but the old dressing has no odor. There is a small amount of serosanguineous drainage on the inner aspect of the dressing. The patient is afebrile and experiences only slight (0–2/10) pain during the dressing change." You would go on to explain the new dressing procedure and sign your note with your name, credentials, date, and time, according to your facility's policies.

Information from the Patient Is Subjective

In the event the patient is reporting something which you think is unsubstantiated, you must report it, but document that the "patient states. . . ." For instance, she is complaining about having 10/10 pain, but exhibits no rise in B/P, pulse, or respirations, is moving freely in bed and able to stand and ambulate without any nonverbal indications such as grimacing or splinting. You would document that "the patient states she is having 10/10 pain in her right thigh region, however she is observed to move freely and actively about in bed and is able to stand and walk ten feet without any verbal or nonverbal expressions of pain such as grimacing or splinting."

Pain is subjective, and indeed the patient might be experiencing this level of pain. However, your documentation of the unrestricted activity also adds to the picture so that the situation can and should be explored with the patient particularly if she is seeking more or higher doses of medication.

One facility may have made it a hard and fast rule that it doesn't divulge a patient's presence in a facility at all. If you called there looking for a relative or friend, such a facility would tell you they cannot tell you if the patient is there. Another hospital requires that the patient officially notify the admitting staff if he wishes to withhold his name from the phone directory. Unless so noted, anyone calling in to ask if the patient is in this facility would be told that he is indeed a patient in this facility.

In most instances, patients do need to designate who can be given information about their care or condition. In the event a patient is not able to consent, it can be implied that next of kin or caregiver be recognized as a designated representative to whom information can be divulged. How the facility's exact policy is written will dictate the actual procedure.

You have an obligation to protect the patient's information from being seen by anyone who has no need to know. That means not leaving electronic records open when you leave your seat by the computer. It means not leaving patient charts out and unattended for anyone to view.

Remember that your patients have public lives as well as private ones. Their neighbor might seem very concerned, but to the patient, she's a nosy gossip-monger. Your patients most likely live in this community. They are teachers and lawyers and real estate agents. The middle school physical education teacher doesn't need to broadcast that he has had prostate surgery; the prominent lawyer has the right to conceal his HIV status; and the award-winning Realtor doesn't need her clients to know she has frequent bouts of Crohn's disease and is considering an ileostomy. Neither do they need to have their idiosyncrasies of coping shared with the community.

Never count on your memory for complete accuracy. Write things down. Don't keep information in your head. Communicate and share what you know. The possibility always exists that you could be called away from your unit, and if you haven't communicated with others, tasks could be mistakenly repeated or omitted.

The patient's safety, well-being, and positive outcomes are your prime objective. Your best proof of what you did and the patient's outcome is in your documentation. You may one day need your documentation to be detailed enough for you to testify without a shadow of your own doubt that everything written is exactly as it happened. You won't be given a chance to supplement or to add your own comments later on. The documentation has to stand on its own.

Part Nine: Staying on Top of Documentation

Take Advantage of Documentation Technology

A PDA (personal digital assistant) may afford you the best possible solution for note-taking. You can set up a new screen for each of your patients in the most basic of notepad software that comes built-in with your PDA.

Your facility may even have the capability of using software that can be synchronized with the main systems to upload from your PDA directly into the hospital's records. This is becoming more common-place especially where computerized record keeping has been utilized for some time.

The advantage of a PDA is that you can protect your files with a password. Even if you misplace your PDA and someone picks it up, he won't have imme-diate access to confidential information. However, you will need to use some type of system to maintain confidentiality in the event that you neglect to delete your notes before you leave for the day with the PDA in your pocket.

You could devise your own system of identifying patients while keeping a large variety of notes on an organized worksheet. A simple means is numbering your patients one through five or six, in order of your assignment.

Whatever system you choose, the more you can customize your work for yourself the more time you can save on the other end. This will ensure that your documentation will be more accurate and timely as well. Don't reinvent the wheel; ask your coworkers if they have something similar that works for them. Perhaps you can brainstorm and come up with something that you could share and duplicate.

Other considerations for your note-taking system include a means to keep the information confidential. You don't want to drop scraps of paper from your pocket in the hospital cafeteria with identifying information on them along with current vital signs or medication notes.

Part Nine: Staying on Top of Documentation

Paperwork Is Just Part of Being a Nurse

Remember always that the medical record is a legal document. It is your proof that you did something. You want the chart to reflect the quality care you have given and you want to protect your nursing license at all times. Accuracy is a vital element. You are providing an annotation of the patient's experience for all other health care team members to refer to in analyzing the patient's progress and outcomes.

Many people feel that the paperwork is an annoyance and insignificant to patient care. The truth is that documentation is one of the most effective means of interdisciplinary communication that the health care delivery system has to offer. In the absence of face-to-face opportunities, the written record affords us perhaps the only form of communication and evidence of the care delivered and the patient's response/outcome.

Documentation does not have to be a dissertation or a thesis, but it needs to include enough information to paint a clear portrait of the events of the shift. Any nurse following you should be able to read your documentation and have an understanding of the patient's condition, as well as the care you provided and how it affected the day's outcomes for that patient.

Don't make charting a chore; it is vital to the continuum of care. Think of it as your chance to prove that you have provided excellent care and that you have made a difference in someone's life today.

Don't make charting a chore; it is vital to the continuum of care. Think of it as your chance to prove that you have provided excellent care and that you have made a difference in someone's life today.

Part Ten

Keep an Eye on Your Future

You will learn something new almost every day of your career. Look for opportunities to keep learning. Even procedures you have now done many hundreds of times can be learning situations if you have an opportunity to assist or observe another nurse. Everyone will develop his own style and process for procedures. What you learn can even be a "how not to do that" situation. Nonetheless, this can be as effective a learning experience as learning something new.

Subscribe to nursing journals and search the Internet for informative sites. Read everything that you can about subjects you feel weak in. If you work on a specialty unit, subscribe to listservs and other e-mail discussion groups or chat rooms for nurses who share your interests and specialty. Join nursing organizations and look for local chapters to attend events and seminars.

Tune in to a news program every day, whether it is on the radio or television. Stay current with political climates and issues that affect your community and the world. Have an understanding of what stimulates and affects your patients' world. Be a responsible citizen of your community. Know what's going on. Keep up-to-date with health care issues in the news and know who and what is effecting changes.

Subscribe to your local newspaper and keep up-to-date on community issues that can impact health care in your area. Doing so can provide you with valuable teaching materials for your patients.

Take the opportunity to attend any workshops, any in-services, and classes offered by your facility. If a seminar is being offered that is applicable to your particular job description or unit, ask your supervisor if you can attend as a representative of your facility.

Become active in your facility by providing your staff educators with ideas and requests for in-services and seminars. Volunteer to sit on committees to choose and run in-services and seminars. As you find valuable resources and information pertinent to your job, share them with your coworkers, and provide a copy to staff educators. They are almost always open to new ideas and subjects.

Sometimes your facility will pay your fees and/or pay you to attend in-services or seminars. You may have to report back to a small group or make a larger presentation to the facility in return, but this can be a terrific opportunity for you to expand your horizons as well.

Part Ten: Keep and Eye on Your Future

Find Opportunities to Improve Your Skills

New techniques and procedures are commonplace in the health care setting. Look for opportunities and ask for a chance to observe and then perform them. Talk to your staff educators and let them know of your interests. Be willing to come in on your own time occasionally to afford yourself a chance to observe and learn.

As you perfect your skills, you will gain confidence and become more and more adept at handling situations. Always strive to keep up your skills, and if you don't have opportunities to perform, be sure to observe and mentally participate. If possible, ask the team to let you try so you can keep up your hands-on skills.

If you work in a teaching facility, you may have much more access and opportunity to observe and practice new techniques and skills. Take advantage of all that is available to you.

Nurses need to use only the latest editions of drug books and ensure that old ones are destroyed. Don't pass them on to your family and friends. There is too much information that changes too rapidly to take a chance that a loved one would refer to an outdated drug book with less-than-optimal results.

Electronic databases from reputable publishers can provide you with the most up-to-date information. Learn to utilize these sources and access Internet pharmacology sites as well. And don't forget to ask the pharmacists. They can and should be your most valuable resource for drug information. That's their job and their field of expertise. They can break down the information into simple nontechnical terms so that you can provide your patients with all the information they need. Pharmacists can also give you some insight into the inside information about drug studies and why certain drugs have been pulled from the market.

Watch for New Treatments and Products

There are always many new safety and assistive devices available to help patients to become more independent and self-reliant. Technological improvements have brought to market multiple at-home testing kits. Glucometers and home pregnancy tests were among the first of these to become popular and essential. Now there are many more that can detect urinary tract infections, coagulation levels, and cholesterol levels, and help to determine when ovulation occurs. Keep your eyes and ears open. At some point, you'll need the information to instruct a patient about such devices.

Depending on how your facility works, you may need to do your own detective work to keep up-to-date on new products. Perhaps no one else has the time to devote to this or wants to take on the responsibility. You could find yourself with a new role.

It's hard to imagine that this could be an issue today, but there are nurses who believe that things don't change that much and that a technique they learned will always be correct. Never expect that what you learned in school will always be correct.

Take, for example, newborns' and infants' sleeping positions. About twenty years ago, the theory was to place infants on their side or abdomen to sleep and to never place them on their backs. In this way, you would avoid any possibilities of aspiration. This was thought to avoid sudden problems such as Sudden Infant Death Syndrome (SIDS). Recently, this whole theory underwent a drastic change, and now the consensus is that infants should only sleep on their backs, to avoid the dangers of suffocation. Now you never place them on their abdomen or side.

Unless an edict from administration demands compliance, some nurses may avoid following new practices because they are uncomfortable with the findings.

Consider Earning an Advanced Degree

Nursing is a field in which you will spend your lifetime learning. You will learn new things almost every day of your career as information and techniques change. Moving to the next level does not always mean moving toward a managerial position. It just means that you need to keep up with the times and accept more or different responsibilities to keep your skills fresh and keep yourself always prepared to make changes as life dictates them to you.

It also means examining where you want to go next with your career. Are you ready to move from a general unit to a more specialized one? Are you ready to obtain the next level of education? Are you an LVN ready to become an RN? Are you an ADN ready to pursue a BSN? Or are you ready to work on a master's or PhD? Furthering your education is an important factor in managing your career.

You may be perfectly satisfied with the level of education you have and the niche you have found. Just keep your eyes, ears, and mind open to new opportunities. Aside from lengthy degree programs, you may find that you want to specialize in an area that the facility is willing to train you for. Internships and other training opportunities can be terrific ways to further your lifelong learning process and can offer you a chance to move into another area or to gain more knowledge and skills for the area you presently work in.

Let your supervisor and staff educators know what your goals are, and enlist their help in obtaining the training necessary to meet the requirements. In addition, you may want to focus your own continuing education units toward meeting your goals as well. Most of all, don't overspecialize, or you may be pigeonholed the rest of your career.

Nurse entrepreneurs are building a huge variety of independent businesses ranging from consultants in many diverse areas of health care to aestheticians to foot care specialists. For many years, nurse practitioners have hung out their own shingles in many fields, such as mental health and women's health. These are expanding now, and it is hoped that Congress will soon recognize the cost savings and other benefits of NPs and will allow for Medicaid reimbursement of their services.

The area of patient education leaves many opportunities for nurses to provide individual and small group instruction on managing disease entities and care issues such as diabetic teaching and managing chronic pain. The job you will hold five years from now probably doesn't even exist today. Be sure to keep your skills current and learn about techniques and diseases beyond your own realm. Keep your options open.

Nursing is one of the most rewarding careers, and at the same time one of the most challenging. By joining professional organizations, you will find that you are not alone in your struggles. You will have a huge network of peers with whom to share your interests and your ideas for helping to make nursing an even better experience for all. You will also have an opportunity to vent and commiserate. Most important, you will be tapped into one of the best sources of information about what's happening in nursing.

Membership gives you clout and makes a statement about your professionalism on a resume. It can give you an edge in competing for a promotion. And you will stay informed of the latest trends in health care issues.

Joining a professional organization is not required, but it is highly recommended. The benefits are many, not the least of which is keeping on top of developments within the profession.

Unfortunately, many people believe that it is only necessary to network with peers when you are looking for a new job. This is only one of the times when you will need to network. The most successful professionals and those who are most satisfied and happy in their jobs find great rewards through constant networking.

Networking includes staying connected with your schoolmates and faculty members. It means spending a meal break with a coworker and getting to know more about him. It means joining listservs to share information about a common issue. In addition, networking means learning about other fields from everyone you encounter personally and professionally.

Next time you attend an in-service or seminar, approach the speaker and exchange business cards. Ask about her role and how she got into this job. You never know when you might be looking for something entirely different to do and may want to contact her again. Stay in touch.

You don't necessarily need a business card that is imprinted with your facility's information; in fact, your boss might think you're being a bit presumptuous to ask for such a thing! All you need is a plain white card imprinted with your name, credentials, and contact information. If you don't want to broadcast your home address, simply include a phone number or even just an e-mail address. You can add a simple graphic such as a stethoscope or an RN emblem, but keep it simple and tasteful. Or use a simple design or color.

There are several computer programs for designing your own cards and printing them from your own computer. These are perfectly acceptable. If you don't have access to this software, there are a number of economical places online and off where you can have simple cards printed for a nominal fee. Always keep them with you and in a business card holder so that they are always clean and crisp. Hand them out!

Part Ten: Keep and Eye on Your Future

Be Actively Involved

Join your professional organizations and become involved. Find a coworker interested in joining or attending local meetings with you. You can attend as a guest. Branch out and meet a new person each time you attend. And share the information with your boss and coworkers.

Become involved with committees at work and let your supervisor know you are interested in volunteering for activities within the facility. Become a preceptor or mentor to the new generation of new grads in your facility or on your unit. Volunteer to help with students when they are assigned to your unit. This will not only provide you with any number of new and interesting experiences, but it will also make you known throughout the facility and even the community as a valuable resource and willing subject. These opportunities will also build your confidence and allow you to measure your success.

Perhaps when considering moving on to the next level, you will find that you would like to explore another area as well. This is part of fine-tuning your career. Keep it interesting and never let it get boring and old.

Making a move will be an exciting challenge as well as a bittersweet one. You will have developed friendships and professional relationships with your coworkers that will be difficult to change and disrupt. However, growth always involves some degree of change. If your career isn't growing, it's most likely stagnating. This can lead to job dissatisfaction and burnout. Stay in touch and ask your colleagues to be happy for you.

If your facility is offering training for the intensive care unit (ICU), and that's where you think you'd like to work someday, then perhaps you should jump at the opportunity. Or perhaps the pediatric ward has an opening, and the unit manager is willing to give you a chance.

150

Focus on What You Love, and Build on Your Strengths

Identify the aspects of your job that you really enjoy and those that you find to be most rewarding. Further identify the skills and talents that you possess and note your strongest and your weakest. Find ways to improve the skills you want to work on.

There are more than enough negative things about nursing; be happy in what you do, and you will be much better at it. If you don't like patients, consider roles where you don't have patient contact. And, of course, if you want more hands-on care, you certainly wouldn't look at positions that take you away from direct interaction with patients.

Re-evaluate your situation periodically, and always stay abreast of new trends in health care and how it will affect your role and the things you enjoy doing most as a nurse. Be open to change and embrace it. Set goals for yourself and specific timelines for achieving them. Be flexible, but don't compromise your needs and success.

Appendix A

Glossary of Terms and Acronyms

ADLs
Activities of daily living: feeding, dressing, hygiene, and mobility.

ADN
Associate's degree nurse: an RN with an associate's degree in nursing.

APN
Advance practice nurse: an RN with an advanced degree or certification.

BSN
Bachelor's of science nurse: an RN with a bachelor's of science degree in nursing.

CCU
Cardiac care unit: a specialized intensive care unit for patients with acute cardiovascular problems. (Can also be known as a critical care unit, which is a generalized intensive care unit.)

CHHA
Certified home heath aide: a nurse's aide who has additional certification in home health care.

CNA
Certified nurse's aide.

Critical Thinking Skills
Ability to use deductive and inductive reasoning to assess and evaluate a situation and make decisions and problem-solve based on your assessment and analysis of the facts.

DOU
Direct observation unit: a step-down care unit; patients who still require monitoring and/or more intense care than a regular med-surg (medical/surgical) unit can provide.

ED
Emergency department.

ER
Emergency room.

GN
Graduate nurse: a nurse who has graduated from an RN program, but has not yet taken or received notice of passing the NCLEX.

ICU
Intensive care unit.

LVN-LPN
Licensed vocational nurse; licensed practical nurse (California and Texas use the term LVN and other states LPN).

MAR
Medication administration record: a list and signed record of medications that a patient has been given.

Med-surg
A medical-surgical unit of a hospital that cares for patients with acute medical problems and/or pre- or post-op surgical patients.

MRSA
Methicillin-resistant staphylococcus aureus.

MSN
Master's of science degreed nurse: an RN with a master's of science degree in nursing.

NA
Nursing assistant.

NCLEX
National council licensure examination: the board exam for nurses that allows for licensure as an LPN/LVN or RN.

NICU
Neonatal ICU: an intensive care unit for infants and premature infants requiring intensive levels of care.

Nosocomial Infection
An infection acquired in a health care facility.

NP
Nurse practitioner: an advanced practice degree for RNs.

NPA
Nurse Practice Act: The group of laws established by each state to protect the public and that define the scope of practice for RNs, APRNs, and LPNs in that state. (RN, APRN, and LPN NPAs are covered in separate documents.) The NPA includes the requirements for education for each level of licensed nurse.

OR
Operating room.

P & P

Policy and procedure: usually refers to a manual detailing the policies and procedures for care and administrative policies as determined by a facility.

PCA

Patient care assistant: an unlicensed person who has had some level of training in bedside patient care as described in the facility's job description.

PHN

Public health nurse: a certificate in public health nursing earned in a BSN program.

PPE

Personal protective equipment: can include gown, gloves, goggles, or face shield, cap and booties to protect against splashing and contamination with bodily fluids and excrement, or other chemical or hazardous materials.

RN

Registered nurse: a nurse who has received training as an RN and has passed the licensure examination.

Scope of Practice

The set of duties and responsibilities that each level of nurse is allowed to perform based on level of education, license they have been granted, and the specific laws and regulations of the state in which the nurse practices.

UAP

Unlicensed assistive personnel: an aide who has been trained by a facility to assist in the care of patients according to a job description devised by the facility.

VRE

Vancomycin-resistant enterococci: an intense strain of bacteria resistant to vancomycin.

Appendix B

Additional Reading

Ball, Sally Perry. "POCT Today: Laboratory Testing at the Bedside Has Had a Significant Positive Impact on Patient Outcomes." Advance for Nurses, 22 August 2005, pp. 30–31.

Cardillo, Donna Wilk. *Your First Year as a Nurse: Making the Transition from Total Novice to Successful Professional.* (Roseville, CA: Prima Publishing, 2001).

Dunham, Kelli S. *How to Survive and Maybe Even Love Nursing School!* (Philadelphia, PA: F. A. Davis Company, 2001).

Eagles, Zardoya E. *Nurses Career Guide: Discovering New Horizons in Health Care.* (San Luis Obispo, CA: Sovereignty Press, 1997).

J. G. Ferguson Publishing Co. *Ferguson's Careers in Focus: Nursing. 2nd edition.* (Chicago, IL: J. G. Ferguson Publishing Co., 2003).

Finkelstein, Barbara, editor. *My First Year as A Nurse: Real World Stories From America's Nurses.* (New York: Signet, 1997).

Munoz, Cora and Hilgenberg, Cheryl. "Ethnopharmocology: Understanding How Ethnicity Can Affect Drug Response Is Essential to Providing Culturally Competent Care." American Journal of Nursing, August 2005, pp. 40–49.

Newell, Robert, editor. *Developing Your Career in Nursing.* (New York: Cassell, 1995).

Rogers, Carla S. *How To Get Into The Right Nursing Program.* (Lincolnwood, IL: VGM Career Horizons, 1998).

Venes, Donald, editor. *Taber's Cyclopedic Medical Dictionary.* (Philadelphia, PA: F. A. Davis Co., 2004).

Appendix C

Websites

Nursing Associations

The following are links to Internet sites for various professional organizations for nurses. Search each site for additional information, resources, and links. For a comprehensive list of specialty nursing associations visit AllNurses.com:

www.allnurses.com/Nursing_Associations/Nursng/USA

American Association of Colleges of Nurses
Educational resources for nurses.

www.aacn.nche.edu/index.htm

American Nurses Association
Professional organization for all nurses in the United States.

http://nursingworld.org

National Association for Practical Nurse Education and Service, Inc.
Professional organization for LPNs and LVNs.

www.napnes.org

National Council for State Boards of Nursing
Links to all State Boards of Nursing. Links to NCLEX testing information for RNs and LPNs.

www.ncsbn.org

National Federation of Licensed Practical Nurses, Inc.
Professional organization for LPNs and LVNs.

www.nflpn.org

National League for Nurses
Organization responsible for the accreditation of nursing education institutions.

www.nln.org

National Organization of Associate Degree Nurses
Professional association for ADNs.

www.noadn.org

National Student Nurses Association
Professional association for student nurses.

www.nsna.org

Nursing Journals and Professional Publications

The following are links to online versions or subscription sources for nursing journals and publications. Some offer online access to archived articles and may provide periodic online newsletters and e-mail updates. This list is by no means complete. There are many more nursing publications available. Search the Internet for nursing journals or nursing publications. A more comprehensive list of publications can be found at the Nursing Center:

www.nursingcenter.com

American Journal of Nursing
www.ajnonline.com

LPN Journal of Practical Nursing
www.napnes.org/journal.htm

Male Nurse Magazine
www.malenursemagazine.com

Nurse Zone
www.nursezone.com

NurseWeek magazine
www.nurseweek.com

Nursing Spectrum
www.nursingspectrum.com

Nursing Weekly
www.nursingweekly.com

RN Magazine
http://rnmodernmedicine.com

Other Useful Websites

The following is a sample of the multitude of nursing websites available that provide resources, information, and forums for nurses to post questions and comments about nursing.

All Nurses
A comprehensive site with forums and links to many resources for nurses, including a list of specialty nurses associations.
www.allnurses.com

The Nursing Site and Blog
http://thenursingsite.com
http://nursingsite.blogspot.com

American Assembly for Men in Nursing
A wealth of information about men in nursing today as well as the history of men in nursing.
www.aamn.org

CollegeBoard.org
Information on SAT and ACT college entrance exams, links to financial aid, and other college entrance information.
www.collegeboard.org

Commission on Graduates of Foreign Nursing Schools
Comprehensive information and instructions for foreign nurses wishing to emigrate to the United States to practice nursing.

www.cgfns.org

Epocrates
A site with information about nursing PDA software databases, includes links to purchase and download the software.

www.epocrates.com

FAFSA (Free Application for Federal Student Aid)
You can access and submit the application online.

www.fafsa.ed.gov

Financial Aid
One of many financial aid information sites.

www.finaid.org

HandHeldMed
A site for nursing PDA software.

www.handheldmed.com

Health Literacy issues
Helen Usborne, a health literacy expert, discusses the issues involving literacy in health care today. Links to many articles and resources.

www.healthliteracy.com

Home Health 101
A site with practical information for home health professionals.

http://homehealth101.com

House Calls Online
A site for home health professionals with links to resources and other home health sites.

http://housecalls-online.com

The Nurses PDR
Online PDR access for nurses for drug information.
www.nursespdr.com

Nursing Center
A comprehensive site with links to journals, publications, nursing websites, and CEUs.
www.nursingcenter.com

NursingNet.com
Many resources and links to nursing information including education and jobs.
www.nursingnet.org

PDR Health
A health resources site.
www.pdrhealth.com

RN.com
Resources including education, jobs, CEUs, and websites.
www.rn.com

RNCentral.com
A site with many sample care plans, a forum, and a library of resources.
www.rncentral.com

Trans Cultural Nursing
Concepts and case studies of cultural diversity issues in nursing.
www.culturediversity.org

Ultimate Nurse
A forum and info site with links to jobs and other nursing sites.
www.ultimatenurse.com

WholeNurse.com
A large database of nursing links for resources, jobs, education, and other nursing sites.
www.wholenurse.com

Index

M

Medications
  communicating with patient about, 102, 104
  discharge and, 109
  "five rights" of, 78
  misinformation about, 101
  staying up-to-date on, 169
Mentors, doctors as, 121

N

Needle sticks, avoiding, 139
Networking, 176
North American Nursing Diagnosis Association (NANDA), 83
Nurse Practice Act (NPA), 7, 9
Nurse practitioners, 11, 174

O

Office politics, 58
On-the job issues, 39–55
Open wounds, sight of, 53
Orientation, to new job, 36–37

P

Paperwork. See Documentation policies
Patients
  accepting "dirty work" of care of, 73
  care plan for, 84
  clinical pathways for care of, 86
  communicating with, 93, 103–9
  death of, 69, 90
  documenting information from, 156
  helping to understand role of nurse, 68
  picturing self as, 89
  questions about your age, 43
  safety and, 79
  smoking odors and, 48
  thinking of "whole" patients, 88, 105
PDAs, 29–30, 33, 160
Perfume, avoiding, 48
Pharmacology. See Medications
Policy and procedure (P&P) manuals, 36, 77
Privacy requests, 101, 157–58
Professionalism
  of all nurses, 15, 18
  appearance and, 46–47
  demeanor and, 10
  opinions and, 118
Professional organizations, joining, 175, 178

R

Reference manuals, 36
Registered Nurse (RN), 2–3
Relaxation techniques, 136
Responsibilities, 1–19
Rights of patients, 101